Presidential
Leadership
Personality and
Political Style

Erwin C. Hargrove
·BROWN UNIVERSITY

The Macmillan Company, New York
Collier–Macmillan Limited, London

First Printing

Library of Congress catalog card number: 66–11579

THE MACMILLAN COMPANY, NEW YORK
COLLIER–MACMILLAN CANADA, LTD., TORONTO, ONTARIO

Printed in the United States of America

Acknowledgments

I owe a debt to all those who have written about the Presidency as an office for the exercise of political skills, especially Richard E. Neustadt, Clinton Rossiter, and Elmer E. Cornwell.

Harold D. Lasswell provided the initial intellectual guidance for those portions of the study that deal with political personality and I wish to thank him. The sharp pencil and critical intelligence of Nelson Polsby provided invaluable editorial assistance. My friend and colleague at Brown, Elmer E. Cornwell, was a constant source of ideas and advice. I have derived more knowledge about the Presidency from him than I can ever repay. I would also like to thank my friend and colleague C. Peter Magrath for reading parts of the manuscript.

Anne Fribourg performed valuable services as a research assistant, and Florence Murphy was an excellent and long-suffering typist.

I would like to thank Robert J. Patterson of The Macmillan Company for his help and encouragement.

Last of all, I want to thank my wife for her patience and support.

E. C. H.

Contents

Presidents of Action and Presidents of Restraint

THIS BOOK is a study of the men who have shaped the modern Presidency. The focus is on their personalities and skills as they have helped or hindered Presidential leadership. Presidents of Action are compared to Presidents of Restraint in terms of the personal drives, skills, and values they have brought to the office, and conclusions are drawn about the consequences of each type of "political personality" and style of leadership for the office.

The three Presidents of Action who have most shaped the Presidential office are the two Roosevelts and Wilson. Each, in his own way, greatly amplified Presidential power. Each was a political artist whose deepest needs and talents were served by a political career. Presidents Truman, Kennedy, and Johnson are considered briefly as Presidents in this tradition.

The Presidents of Restraint—Taft, Hoover, and Eisenhower—went to the White House from careers as non-political technicians. They did not put a high value on personal or Presidential power, and in the course of their careers they did not develop political skills. Their values were hostile to strong Presidential leadership, to the manipulation of others, to popular emotion, and to politics in general.

American political culture contains two important and conflicting views of the Presidency. The Whig theory, seen in the Presidents of Restraint, is almost an anti-theory, for it preaches that the incumbent should deliberately exercise restraint on his power and influence. It was shaped out of a fear of a strong, popular Presidency. This tradition does not value political skill in the President but rather stresses rectitude and dignity.

The irony is that such a view of the Presidency impedes an effective discharge of Presidential tasks. A sense of power and the willingness to search for it and use it with political skill are essential today.

The other tradition calls for strong Presidential leadership, for

1

the Presidency to be the agency of popular reform. However, within this tradition the Presidents of Action who reflect it must continually do battle with those in Congress and the public who hold to the opposing model of Presidential leadership. The Presidents of Action often cause counterreactions that may eventually throw up Presidents of Restraint.

This lack of congruence between the political culture and the central political office exists in none of the other English-speaking democracies. It is in part a function of the dual nature of the Presidential office which is that of both a national symbol and a partisan leader. It also reflects differing views of the importance of government action. Progressives favor Presidential leadership and conservatives are skeptical of it.

Almost all students of the modern Presidency agree that the President today must be strong and skillful in his leadership of public opinion, of Congress, and of the bureaucracy beneath him. Skill has two components: a sensitivity to power relationships and the ability to act to maximize personal, that is, Presidential, power in each of these areas. The President has relatively little formal power to win compliance for his policies from publics, Congress, or administrators. He must find informal ways to persuade them to support him and this requires political skill.

A set of explicit norms for the conduct of each of these Presidential roles runs throughout this book. The Presidents are compared and judged in terms of the capacity their political personalities and, therefore, their skills give them to play these roles.

It is assumed that the President must lead and educate public opinion. It is his chief source of power in Washington in his dealings with other holders of power. He needs technical skill, for example, speaking ability, a sense of timing, and empathy for public moods. But, more than this, he needs the ability and will to fit his policy leadership to an over-all strategy of leadership of public opinion. He must put events and policies in context and must gradually prepare the public for new departures. He must not continually lay his reputation on the line without success, but he must try to lead if he wants to be effective. If the President did not articulate the needs of the nation our democracy would be poorer.

All Presidents are now expected to be legislative leaders. Congress requires such leadership in order to be effective in its operation because it is not organized to lead. However, the internal organization and processes of Congress and the perspectives of its members, which are so different from those of the White House, present real obstacles to Presidential legislative leadership. He can use his messages, his budget, bills drafted in the executive branch, the veto power, and open appeal to the people as levers against Congress. He can also use patronage, the pork barrel, personal persuasion, accommodation and compromise, and the extraction of agreement out of collective bargaining. He must never cease to press for action and yet he cannot seem to dominate for fear of injuring Congressional pride. It is a job for a man who delights in the political process.

The President has difficulty in controlling the federal executive because of its size, variety, and complexity and the fact that much of it is independent of him in law and in fact because of long-established ties with Congress. He cannot simply issue commands and expect compliance within his own branch. He cannot count on receiving the information he needs from official channels. Officials beneath him are always tempted to go into business for themselves and to tell him only what they want him to know. In addition, they are not likely to see what he needs to know. The President must ensure that the essential decisions of state remain in his hands and he must also ensure that he receives the information necessary for such decisions, as well as seeing that the decisions are implemented once they are made. Thus, he needs as many sources of information as possible, including unofficial channels. And he must so organize his administration that the major decisions come to him and he can make his presence felt throughout bureaucracy as a galvanizing force. There is no one form of organization that will do all these things, but the test of Presidential skill in administration is his sensitivity and response to these inherent problems.

It is contended here that the first requisite for doing these tasks well is a sense of personal—and thus, Presidential—power. This sense of power is a function of "political personality," which is an amalgam of the drives, values, and traits of the leader. It is our premise that the skills of leadership are rooted in political personality.

The model of political personality used in this study contains four variables: needs, mental traits, values, and the ego, or unifying agent, which joins the first three factors into a recognizable personality. In practice these variables so interlace that they cannot be separated and this is the value of the concept of "ego integration." We avoid the error of reducing our explanations of behavior to any one factor. The personality acts as a unity.[1]

We do not see "needs." They are constructs inferred from observation of behavior. A leader who continually seeks attention in private and public life is said to have a need for attention that his dramatizing behavior serves. Needs and mental qualities, of course, fuse together but our use of the latter term is a common sense one. Does a man's mind seem to have been logical and rigorous or illogical, impressionistic, and empathetic? Did he feel at home in flux or seek ordered relationships? It is obvious that mental traits may reflect needs or may have been instrumental in the development of some needs over others. This is a chicken–egg question. Certainly, mental traits serve needs and from the combination abilities develop. It is postulated that leaders seek to gratify their needs in the playing of political roles. They find some roles more congenial than others and shape roles to fit their predispositions of need, mentality, and ability.

The category of political values, or ideology, has two components: beliefs about policy and beliefs about proper behavior of the leader. Ideology is often congruent with needs and abilities. It cannot be reduced to a projection of personality needs. In the process of personal development, needs and mental traits shape abilities and all of these blend with a congenial set of values, which in turn help shape needs and mental traits. The edges of each factor are softened so that all can live together in varying degrees of comfort. The ego is the component of personality that organizes and directs these forces and mediates between them and the world. We shall assume in this study that political acts are most often a compound of several levels of political personality. It is interesting that these levels seem to reinforce each other as factors in motivation.

The choices that go into political artistry are rooted in stable predispositions, and in this sense they are intuitive as much as they are calculated. The situation helps shape the strategy and tactics of leadership but the skill in strategy or tactics is likely to be summoned forth from the reservoir of the unconscious. Most people who are quite good at something do not know why it is so. They work hard to refine their talent but the talent originally existed. Neustadt contends

---

[1] This model is drawn from Henry Murray's theory of needs, Henry A. Murray, *Explorations in Personality* (New York: Oxford University Press, 1938), and from the concept of the ego as an integrating mechanism in M. Brewster Smith, Jerome S. Bruner, and Robert W. White, *Opinions and Personality* (New York: John Wiley and Sons, 1956).

that the choices that go into the pursuit of Presidential "power" are a function of "perception," that is, whether or not the President is sensitive to power relationships, both potential and actual.[2] Perception is a function of personality. Some people are more sensitive to power relationships than others because of the differences in their unconscious adaptive mechanisms, implicit values, mental qualities, goals, and so forth.

In this study a biographical approach is used to describe political personality. We can see it develop in early life until a relatively consistent set of adult patterns exist. The method of analysis is to look for recurring patterns of skill and strategies of leadership and to relate them to political personality. Of course, situational and institutional factors must also be taken into account. But, Presidential personality, as an independent variable, has been neglected by political scientists, although not by historians and biographers.

This book is not a study of political biography for its own sake, but rather, it is an attempt to learn more about the qualities of personality required for the staggering tasks of the Presidency. The temperament and skills of one man are more important today than ever before. If we begin our analyses with consideration of the characters of private men, we finish with conclusions about their impact on public office.

In a sense, the Presidential office is shapeless, and each President fills it out to suit himself. Personality is certainly the chief factor. But, in another sense, the office has continuity in that succeeding Presidents make permanent contributions to the institution itself in the form of precedents of behavior or new powers. This has been particularly true of the Presidents of Action. Theodore Roosevelt created the modern Presidency as an agency of popular government. Woodrow Wilson institutionalized the President as chief legislator. Franklin D. Roosevelt provided the model of the President as an administrator of a giant bureaucracy. The Presidents of Restraint were generally reluctant to create these kinds of precedents. By holding to the Whig theory they fought against the tendency to make the office an agency of popular reform. This is a losing fight. It raises the possibility that the Presidency may not be a congenial place for American conservatives.

There are three levels of analysis and comparison in this book.

[2] Richard E. Neustadt, *Presidential Power* (New York: John Wiley and Sons, Inc., 1960).

We compare political personalities and assess the consequences of different kinds of personalities for style and skill. In this regard we also compare political subcultures, since each set of leaders embodies a different subculture. We compare these types of political personality in the playing of Presidential roles, and again assess the consequences, and, finally, we assess the impact of each type on the Presidency itself.

PART ONE

Introduction

THE TWO ROOSEVELTS and Wilson shaped the modern Presidency and we shall look at the institutional contributions of each in detail. Our theme here is the qualities they had in common that made them political "masters." Their political skill was the primary factor in their policy achievements and their impact on the Presidency. They developed a tradition of skill and a set of ground rules for Presidential effectiveness that have greatly influenced succeeding Presidents of Action. In fact, they influenced each other. Wilson took his ideas of strong Presidential leadership, in part, from the example of Theodore Roosevelt in office. Franklin Roosevelt admired and copied both "Uncle Ted" and Wilson, whom he served. What characteristics of political personality did they have in common?

1. They were driven by the need for personal power and this was the initial reason for their choice of a political career. In each man the quality of the need to influence and direct others was different but this kind of drive is essential to great political skill.

2. Their needs seems to have stimulated them to develop their abilities to influence others. In their youth and early careers they gradually shaped themselves into effective leaders in response, not to their policy ideals, but to their inner imperatives, that is, the needs for power and attention.

The developing relationships between needs, natural abilities, and skills of leadership are charted in each chapter. An example of this interaction would be Theodore Roosevelt's dramatizing ability. A need for attention seemed to be at the root of this skill, and out of that need acting and self-dramatizing talents were developed. Perhaps the talents stimulated the need. This is not important. What is important is that this private skill was eventually used for political goals. Roosevelt served his own need for attention while he served his goals for achievement. We can see in each of these men that beneath the threshold of public action there was a second level of private need, that is, to influence others, that was always pushing, reinforcing, and guiding their public actions. The private need increased their public effectiveness. These private needs cannot be explained by their public roles. They antedated these roles and reinforced them.

3. Mental traits, another component of political personality, also contributed to political skill. In each case, qualities of mind and of temperament fitted together, for example, Franklin Roosevelt was empathetic and intuitive in his human relations and flexible and an empiricist in his mode of thinking. As we shall see, this congruence was important for the performance of Presidential roles. Needs and drives and intellectual qualities gave these men a sensitivity to power relationships.

4. Values gave them a sense of purpose in the Presidency that increased their effectiveness as leaders. Technical skill alone would not have been enough to account for their policy achievements. They came to office in periods of American history when there was need for national innovation and a redefinition of national goals. All were equal to the task. The fact that they were all "cultural outsiders" to American business civilization may help to explain their role as reformers. The two Roosevelts were aristocrats with roots in a pre-industrial way of life. Wilson, a Southerner by birth and upbringing, and an academic by profession, was also an outsider in his era. Each man, therefore, found one variety or another of progressivism congenial because of its criticism of the values and practices of a business civilization. However, they had "conservative" roots as well. They were not radicals but rather reformers who were well equipped to be brokers between the past and future. They were also "marginal men" who lived and worked in several American worlds without being fully committed to any particular world. This gave them a perspective for the role of broker leaders.

5. Each man was favored by the times in which he became President. This was less true of Theodore Roosevelt than the other two, and his achievements were correspondingly less. But, in all three instances, skills of leadership were most effective when supported by favorable situations.

6. Their strengths were also their weaknesses. The same intense drives that sent them into political life and accounted for their skill and success were also their undoing at times. Theodore Roosevelt kept restraint on his ruder impulses while in the White House because he loved and gloried in the job. Out of office, at a relatively young age, he was unhappy and frustrated because his talents had no outlet. His subsequent bid to return to power smashed his own party and ruined his political career. Woodrow Wilson built many of his successes on

his moral rigidity and refusal to compromise. But, in the fight for Senate approval of the League of Nations, his rigidity defeated him. Franklin Roosevelt's self-confidence was a source of national strength in time of crisis, but in the fight to pack the Supreme Court it betrayed him. There was a tragic flaw in the character of each of these men that was bound up with their talent. However, their darker qualities were not harmful to democratic institutions. When these drives got out of control they were self-defeating. The man and his policies suffered but American institutions were not harmed. The most important restraints on the drive for power, in each case, were not institutional but personal. They could not have succeeded as democratic leaders without self-control and conscience and belief in democracy as a way of life.

7. The unique contribution of each man to the institution of the Presidency was a consequence of his political personality. They shaped Presidential roles in ways that were congenial to them.

CHAPTER 1

Theodore Roosevelt:
The Dramatizing Leader

ROOSEVELT came to the Presidency in 1901 at a time when the wave of popular reform that was to become the progressive movement was just beginning. His arrival also coincided with the development of mass circulation newspapers and popular magazines. Before this time the office of President had been rather passive, and it was Roosevelt's achievement to seize upon these new trends to make the Presidency an agency for popular reform. His urge to dramatize himself and his love of being in the midst of action caused him to bring himself, the Presidency, and his reform policies to the center of national attention in a way that no other President had done. He was peculiarly a dramatizing President. This was his contribution to the office, to make it, in his words, "a bully pulpit." He did it in the same way that he had conducted himself in all of his previous offices, by self-dramatization. His lasting contribution to the institution was the creation of the precedent of the Presidency as the vehicle for the articulation of popular reform.

He came before the full wave of reform but he helped to build it up by his preaching, and Woodrow Wilson was the eventual beneficiary. Although his legislative achievements were not numerous, he was the first modern President to show how a preaching, dramatizing President could express the popular demand for reform and use public opinion as a lever to win action in Congress. He was also a pioneer in the use of Presidential public relations techniques. The modern Presidential press conference began with him.

He had a great need for power and pursued it with purpose and intensity. In every office that he held he delighted in the joys of leadership. He set a model for later Presidents to follow in his fine art of knowing the nature of Presidential power and its strengths and limitations. His letters, which run to several volumes, are filled with practical political wisdom about ways of acquiring Presidential influence, with publics, legislators, and bureaucracy.

In terms, then, of both drama and power he modernized the

Presidency by seeking to perform all Presidential tasks to the hilt. The key to his political style was drama: he was a dramatic person, a dramatic leader of public opinion, a dramatic legislative and administrative leader. In every role he worked to impose his personality with maximum impact and to achieve the greatest dramatic effect. We shall begin by looking at the roots of his political personality, the roots of his dramatizing skills.

Personality Needs

There was strong exhibitionism in Roosevelt's character. His letters, his casual comments, and his exhibitionist behavior reveal an insecurity. He once told his military aide that he envied Taft because people liked Taft at first sight, whereas "I have always got to overcome a little something before I get to the heart of people." [1] This was not actually true, but he devised a thousand dramatizing techniques to overcome this imaginary barrier. He was aided in winning over people by his striking personal magnetism about which all who knew him testified. This magnetism seemed to be a combination of energetic vitality, striking physical appearance, and dramatic gifts, all of which he deliberately exploited in a way that overwhelmed others.

His military aide, Archie Butt, noticed this same magnetism:

. . . one never gets away from Mr. Roosevelt's personality . . . so when he comes into a room and stands as he always does for one second before doing something characteristic, he electrifies the company . . .[2]

His love of costumes was one clue to his exhibitionism. His cowboy outfits in the Badlands belonged in a circus. He wrote a friend in 1884 that in his special cowboy suit, including his revolver and rifle, "I feel able to face anything." [3] He had himself photographed frequently in his cowboy clothes and his Rough Rider uniform.

As Police Commissioner of New York he prowled the streets at night in evening clothes and an opera cape and wore a black sash to the office in the daytime.

A craving for popularity and fear that the public might desert him in their affections appears constantly throughout his letters. He

[1] Archie Butt, *The Letters of Archie Butt,* ed. Lawrence F. Abbott (New York: Doubleday and Co., 1924), p. 233.
[2] Butt, *The Letters of Archie Butt,* p. 233.
[3] Henry F. Pringle, *Theodore Roosevelt* (New York: Harcourt, Brace and World, 1931), p. 97.

was convinced that he would lose every election he fought, and between elections he constantly saw his support eroding. Even when
his popularity seemed to be high he was predicting a violent reaction
against him as inevitable.

In 1884 after a series of legislative triumphs in the New York
Assembly he wrote:

I realize very thoroughly the absolutely ephemeral nature of the hold
I have upon the people.[4]

As Governor of New York he was convinced that he could not be
reelected and when he was nominated for Vice-President he wrote:

. . . do not get mistaken about my strength. This popularity of mine
is in its very nature evanescent.[5]

These anxieties were always out of proportion to the real situation. After he won a smashing victory in 1904 he could write:

But don't you be mislead by the fact that just at the moment men are
speaking well of me. They will speak ill soon enough.[6]

This insecurity drove him to develop the political skills and appeals
that would give him the public approval he craved. His frequent
assertions of certain failure were simply a case of protesting too much.

In every boy's biography of Theodore Roosevelt the point is made
that he was sickly as a youth and he compensated for his weakness
by building up his body, an example of compensatory striving. This
was the initial source of his lifelong habits of shooting, hunting,
riding, rowing, wrestling, boxing, swimming, tennis, ju-jit-su, his
reveling in the life of the cowboy and the soldier, and his many
broken bones and narrow escapes with death. The cultivation of the
strenuous life was common among men of Roosevelt's class and
generation but he was extreme. Richard Hofstadter notes that T. R.
could never find a "saturation point." Who else had been a cowboy,
Rough Rider, President, taker of the Panama Canal, historian, and
so forth?

If all this was supposed to induce a sense of security it seems to have
failed badly. At the age of sixty he was still waving the flag and screaming
for a regiment. One can only suspect that he was fleeing from some more

---

[4] Theodore Roosevelt, *The Letters of Theodore Roosevelt,* ed. Elting E.
Morison (8 vols.; Cambridge: Harvard University Press, 1951–1954), I, p. 66.

[5] Roosevelt, *Letters,* II, p. 1356.

[6] Roosevelt, *Letters,* IV, p. 1328.

persistent sense of deficiency than that induced by the obvious traumatic experiences of his childhood. He fled from repose and introspection with a desperate urgency that is sometimes pitiable.[7]

He was a perennial military volunteer, especially during periods of lag in his political career. He realized his dream with the Rough Riders in the war with Spain. Years later he told his military aide:

I know now that I would have turned from my wife's deathbed to answer that call. It was my chance to cut my little knotch on the stick that stands as the measuring rod in every family.[8]

The greatest disappointment of his career was President Wilson's denial of his request to lead troops in France during World War I. He needed to surround himself with evidence of his prowess, as seen in his favorite room at Sagamore Hill, the North Room, which was crammed with the heads of animals he had brought down, his relics of war, and so forth.

Roosevelt was driven by inner forces to demonstrate his virtuosity and the same dynamic was seen in his ambition for political office. Just as he was usually convinced that popularity was deserting him, so was he fearful that each office would be his last. His letters are filled with predictions that he would be able to go no higher in politics, even though he was always angling for a higher post. When he became Vice-President he simultaneously wrote friends that his political career was finished, began to work to round up delegates for his own nomination for the Presidency four years in advance, volunteered for service in a New York regiment should war occur and vowed to study law since his return to private life was a certainty.

Roosevelt reveled in the exercise of power. This was another way of testing himself, another form of compensatory striving. Out of these "testing" drives he developed the skills that made him a leader of power. Roosevelt himself wrote:

I love the White House; I greatly enjoy the exercise of power.[9]

He sought power over others with the same single-minded intensity with which he sought popularity and prowess. His letters during his early career as Civil Service Commissioner, Police Commissioner, and Assistant Secretary of the Navy revealed his love of power:

[7] Richard Hofstadter, *The American Political Tradition* (New York: Vintage Books, 1948), p. 210.

[8] Butt, *The Letters of Archie Butt*, p. 146.

[9] Roosevelt, *Letters*, VI, p. 1329.

My two colleagues are out of town now, so I am getting my own sweet will with the Civil Service Commission. I much enjoy it; and I really get through much more work than when they are here.[10]

I am getting the Police Department under control; I forced Byrnes and Williams out and now hold undisputed sway.[11]

The Secretary is away, and I am having immense fun running the Navy.[12]

Mental Traits

T. R. had great verbal skill. An estimated 100,000 letters that he wrote are available today. In 1886 he wrote a biography of Thomas Hart Benton in four months although he worked fourteen hours a day on his ranch. In the five-year period after that time he wrote seven volumes of history and essays while active in both politics and ranching.

His memory was photographic. He easily remembered names and faces, often recognizing people by name or face years after only one meeting.

He had extraordinary ability to coin slogans: "speak softly and carry a big stick," "strenuous life," "muckraker," "malefactors of great wealth," "lunatic fringe," "square deal," and "my hat is in the ring" all originated spontaneously with T. R.

He had omnivorous intellectual interests. He read widely and sought acquaintance with people from all intellectual fields and all walks of life. He was always in search of new experiences. He had a highly developed empathy in his dealings with others. When he met people he gave them the instant impression that he liked them. He knew how to draw them out about their interests and needs. His curiosity and need to make conquests came together.

Values and Ideology

In his youth Roosevelt developed a body of guiding principles that he adhered to all of his life.[13] The first component was a view of life as a struggle. Its origins were in his nature studies, Darwinian theories,

[10] Roosevelt, *Letters,* I, p. 245.
[11] Roosevelt, *Letters,* I, p. 459.
[12] Roosevelt, *Letters,* I, p. 655.
[13] John M. Blum, *The Republican Roosevelt* (Cambridge: Harvard University Press, 1954), Ch. 3, "The Roots of Conviction," *passim.* Elting E. Morison, Introduction, *The Letters of Theodore Roosevelt,* V, *passim.*

and his boyhood neurosis about strenuosity. But, he was never a thoroughgoing Darwinian who believed in survival of the fittest as a first and sole principle. Rather, he was an aristocrat by birth who received from his father and his father's friends a sense of *noblesse oblige* for the less fortunate.

Unlike many of his contemporaries who accepted the Darwinian thesis with an optimistic sense of automatic progress, Roosevelt saw life as a chaos with only two certainties, birth and death. Life lay between, as a series of unstable situations on which man impressed a purpose by action. Roosevelt's response to this fact was to develop a code of life that joined the flux of process and struggle with the canons of morality in an effort to make life work and hold society together. He assumed that society was made up of unstable, conflicting forces and was always in danger of breaking down. The task of politics was to reconcile opposing elements in a fragile equilibrium through compromise. His speeches are filled with the conflicts of American life between farm and city, worker and company, and so forth. He saw the "Square Deal" as an equilibrium in which opposing groups were joined by a series of compromises. The role of government was to redress injustices on all sides and replace the jungle with law and order.

His aristocratic origins made him dislike the predatory economic practices of the Rockefellers and the Vanderbilts. Similarly, he had contempt for corrupt machine politicians who were allied with men of wealth. He developed a belief in the power of government and a vigorous executive, to curb the excesses of economic power in American life and to provide a countervailing power against legislatures, which he saw as agencies of delay and corruption.

Political Personality

All of these beliefs committed him to a political style that was based on operational skills. If the goal was to create equilibrium out of potential chaos and to do it through forms of struggle, a premium was put on the political leader who had the skills to bring order out of chaos. There was a unity between Roosevelt's view of the mission of politics and his own need for striving that drove him to extract attention, approval, and power from the responses of others. He made himself into a political artist, skilled at bringing men together in temporary compromises. He built a world view that was congenial to those needs, but those needs were also subordinated to his values.

Drives for power had to be harnessed to a politics of compromise and a higher moral purpose.

This operational approach to existence permitted Roosevelt to develop highly his intuitive sense. He had a more accurate feeling for the tensions and problems of social and economic life in America than any man of his time. It was he who first summoned middle class morality against the abuses of big business. He perhaps believed in and exalted power too much, but he consciously sought to limit his abuse of it by personal character and by limiting the duration of power. Thus, he retired in 1909 even though he wanted to continue as President. He believed that law, morality, and the limitation of tenure, as well as the expert advice that he sought on all issues, were sufficient checks on his power. He thus felt free to use his limited power to the hilt to achieve his objectives.

In his early posts he gradually acquired a self-restraint over his more imperious impulses and developed political skills and experience for the leadership that was to come. As Civil Service Commissioner and Police Commissioner he was impetuous, belligerent, and often contemptuous of the necessities of compromise in politics and of working through a political party. By the time he became Governor he had developed a realistic operational style, in which he sought to get along with the political machine that had nominated him and yet push hard for reform. His notable achievements as Governor came when he carried popular opinion with him against the wishes of the machine, but he never completely alienated his party. He learned to compromise in order to achieve his goals and developed the skills of power in managing a party, leading public opinion, dramatizing issues, and dominating the policy-making process. Upon becoming President in 1901 at age forty-three, Roosevelt was ready for the great challenge.

Conception of the Presidency

T. R. never really believed in checks and balances. Franklin Roosevelt loved to tell the story in later years of visiting the White House and hearing his Presidential cousin scream in exasperation at the failure of a bill: "Oh, if I could only be President and Congress too for just ten minutes." [14] As Civil Service and Police Commissioner he had not enjoyed being the chairman of collegial groups and had sought always to dominate his colleagues.

[14] Frank Freidel, *Franklin D. Roosevelt: The Apprenticeship* (Boston: Little, Brown and Company, 1952), p. 86.

As President he developed a "stewardship" theory of the Presidency under which the President, as the representative of all the people, had the obligation to use his power and prestige to the fullest in behalf of the national interest as he saw it. The President could act in any sphere, he felt, no matter how unprecedented, so long as the Constitution did not forbid it. This was in contrast to the prevailing conservative theory, later held by Taft, that the President could not act without explicit authorization. In 1908, looking back, T. R. wrote a friend:

> While President I have been President, emphatically; and have used every ounce of power there was in the office and I have not cared a rap for the criticisms of those who spoke of my "usurpations of power"; for I knew that the talk was all nonsense and that there was no usurpation.[15]

Leader of Public Opinion

Roosevelt knew the political value of self-advertisement and he enjoyed being in the spotlight. His news sense and dramatic flair explain how the practice began of treating the President and his family as the subject of color stories of interest to the general reader.[16]

In the White House he continued to do many things that he had always done but now they attracted attention. He took ambassadors and generals for "obstacle-course" walks in Rock Creek Park. He attacked Jack London and other "nature fakers" for their false portrayal of animal life. He got into a controversy by suddenly directing that "simplified spelling" be used in all government documents. When the military grumbled about an exercise order he had issued, he executed it himself in a ride to Warrenton, Virginia, and back in a blizzard. These antics endeared him to the American people. They felt, contagiously, what a New York policeman who had served under him once described as "the fun of him."

He worried constantly about his public image and took infinite pains to shape it. A Mississippi bear hunt was a failure in 1902 and the cartoonists had good fun with teddy bears eluding the Presidential hunting party. Always after that Roosevelt would not go hunting unless his hosts would guarantee him that he would get a bear, or a lion. In 1905 he wrote the following:

---

[15] Roosevelt, *Letters,* VI, p. 1087.
[16] Elmer E. Cornwell, *Presidential Leadership of Public Opinion* (Bloomington: Indiana University Press, 1965), p. 9.

The first bear must fall to my rifle. . . . this sounds selfish but you know the kind of talk there will be in the newspapers about such a hunt, and if I go it must be a success, and the success must come to me.[17]

Roosevelt had much reason to thank the cartoonists. They enhanced his color by drawing him in his many costumes and roles: the cowboy and Rough Rider suits, poised with a "big stick" over the dome of Congress, showing his full mouth of teeth in the magnificent grimace that was his grin. They made a colorful man even more colorful.

Use of the Press

Roosevelt was his own press agent in the White House. James Pollard said:

His personal magnetism, his flair for the dramatic, his gift of tongues, his capacity for finding common ground with diverse elements of the public, and his very impulsiveness, all combined to make him the darling of the working newspaperman.[18]

He was the first President to create press offices in the White House for reporters. He had frequent off the record news conferences with them in which he would provide background or let out trial ballons, that is, statements that would be printed without attribution as to source, to test their political usefulness. He often revealed information confidentially to newsmen that would undercut opposition in Congress. For example, when the general counsel of Standard Oil sent telegrams to a few senators urging them to oppose a measure, Roosevelt told reporters that John D. Rockefeller had sent the wires. This made better copy than the attorney's name and it caused a public uproar.

He never permitted news to be given out from the White House without his approval and he usually gave it out personally, often himself suggesting the idea for the lead. Several reporters believed that he would have been a great city editor because of his nose for news and his empathy for what the public would like to read. T. R. saw the ebbing of the editorial and the growing importance of the news headline and the cartoon and he tailored his actions accordingly.

He knew all the personnel of the mass circulation magazines and by personal diplomacy with these journalists he kept these magazines full of articles praising his crusades.[19]

[17] Pringle, *Roosevelt*, p. 345.
[18] James E. Pollard, *The Presidents and the Press* (New York: The Macmillan Company, 1947), p. 569.
[19] Cornwell, *Presidential Leadership*, p. 16.

Roosevelt was the first President to use the Presidential junket as a calculated publicity device. For example, in 1907 he made a trip down the Mississippi River with the members of the Inland Waterways Commission, in a manner which, as he wrote, attracted "wide public attention" and gave the Waterways a new standing in public esteem. At Memphis he announced, with much fanfare, that he would call a White House conference on the conservation of natural resources. Reporters went along on this trip.

On these junkets he took great delight in showing himself to the people. Archie Butt remembered that T. R. would rush to the window or the rear of the train at a stop or crossing if even a handful of people gathered. Once, the nearsighted President found himself waving frantically at a herd of cows. He also used tours for the purpose of educating the public. In 1902 he made a long national speaking tour. His speeches reveal that T. R. was preparing the public for programs to come, for example, a larger fleet, conservation, and regulation of business.[20] In this way great numbers of people could become familiar with ideas that they were not likely to read.

Roosevelt's battle for the passage of the Hepburn Act, which increased regulation of railroad rates, illustrates his great skill in public relations. He waited until after his great victory of 1904 when his popularity would be at its height. His sensitive antenna told him it was the proper time to strike at the railroads. Middle class morality, as expressed in the popular magazines, was up in arms about abuses in railroad rates. Farmers' organizations were calling for government ownership. Southern and Western state legislatures were demanding that Congress act. Roosevelt decided to bring these protests to a head. His main task was to win support for the bill in the Senate. His chief dramatic weapon was himself—on the stump. He began in early 1905 and spoke around the country for the next eighteen months until Congress finally passed the bill. He spoke at Chautauqua, in Chicago, before the Texas legislature, and campaigned for the bill in the Middle West and Southwest en route to the Rough Riders reunion in Texas, where, of course, he received much publicity. In the fall of 1905 he visited his mother's home in Georgia, and exhibited his great capacity to blend with the local scenery. He praised Confederate leaders, mentioned his own Southern blood, and called for railroad legislation. An astonished reporter wrote that it was as if Roosevelt:

[20] Addison O. Thomas, *Roosevelt Among the People* (Chicago: The P. W. Walter Company, 1910), *passim*.

. . . himself fired the last two shots from the Alabama instead of his uncle. . . . Wherever the President's visit is discussed, you will hear men who believed in and fought for the Confederate cause speak of him with the affection of a comrade.[21]

It was also good for the Hepburn Act. In Washington he kept up the drumfire by calling impromptu press conferences on key provisions of the bill. He directed that federal agencies keep releasing news items about the railroad problem. One headline, appearing on December 11, 1905, read: "Attorney-General Moody Directs All United States Attorneys to Prosecute All Railroads Shown to be Giving Rebates." [22] As the campaign increased, the Roosevelt-inspired headlines increased. In this instance Roosevelt brought all of his dramatizing skills to bear: his feeling for public opinion, his ability to create news, his good relations with reporters, and his ability to carry a case to the country on a speaking tour.

Strategic Use of Drama

Other things being equal, T. R. usually tried to choose a dramatic issue instead of a dull one. He chose to prosecute the most unpopular trusts and at the point of weakest legal link to be sure of winning. He wanted dramatic victories, sometimes at the sacrifice of substance. In his judgment the dramatic act was the best entering wedge for long-term reform.

In 1902 Roosevelt, through his attorney general, made the surprising announcement that the government would initiate an anti-trust suit against the Northern Securities Company, a railroad monopoly that had been created by the collusion of J. P. Morgan, James J. Hill, and E. H. Harriman. It was an unsavory deal and the new company threatened shippers in the upper Middle West with monopoly rates. This new company was not the key element of either Hill's or Harriman's empire, but it was legally vulnerable and had the odium of unpopularity. It was a paper creation, not long formed, and therefore easy to dissolve. Furthermore, it was a good way for Roosevelt to make clear a new departure in anti-trust policies. It was characteristic of his dramatic sense.

Roosevelt always kept an eye to the dramatic possibilities of his actions. He helped settle the anthracite coal strike in the winter of 1903 by personally intervening in the negotiations between workers

[21] William Henry Harbaugh, *Power and Responsibility: The Life and Times of Theodore Roosevelt* (New York: Farrar, Straus and Cudahy, 1961), p. 241.
[22] Cornwell, *Presidential Leadership,* p. 25.

and owners in an unprecedented manner. He chose to prosecute the beef trust, which was surely the most unpopular of all trusts. He sent the fleet around the world in a gesture calculated to dramatize the American navy to the American public as well as to the world, especially the Japanese.

One could not claim that T. R.'s unconscious needs for attention and approval were the sole root of his dramatizing style. These needs probably did spur him to develop and use his dramatizing skills, but so did the objective role in which he found himself. His dramatic abilities enabled him to play that role well, and to draw political capital from it.

Roosevelt's genius was that he was able to anticipate and articulate the half-expressed wishes of the majority of Americans. His Square Deal was not a systematic theory or program. Rather, it was a vague, middle position between radicalism and reaction, and this was what most Americans seemed to want. This of course matched his own world view, his desire for uneasy equilibrium. But he found this middle ground by politics, by his great intuitive feeling for what the majority wanted.

Legislative Leader

All of the facets of Roosevelt's political personality were brought to bear in his leadership of Congress: his dramatic skills, his love of manipulating others, his sense of balance and of politics as the art of the possible, and his nervous anxieties, which drove him to make conquests of others. His style of leadership, based on mastery of the political process, was congenial to one whose political theory was preoccupied with operations and operating principles, rather than with schematic principles.

Because he came to the White House in the years when the progressive movement was just beginning he did not have a great ground swell of popular opinion behind him with which to confront Congress. As much as any man he helped to bring progressive opinion to the surface, to articulate it, and to inspire it with passion. His task of legislative leadership was to create the opinion that he would use as a lever against a reluctant Congress. Since the times were good and discontent was not yet general, he had to pick his issues carefully, educate the public as he went along, and strike only when confident of victory. Therefore, he was cautious and diplomatic with Congress, but at the same time the leaders were always afraid of him. He was unpredictable and they could never be sure of the risks of defying him.

Upon first becoming President he did not act to undercut the congressional leaders, even though Leader of the Senate majority Aldrich and Speaker Cannon were of the Republican Old Guard and unsympathetic to him. He knew he could not work without them, and he decided to use them. However, he seldom let them use him. He knew how to work with them and bring pressure to bear on them at the same time.

We see here a paradox about Roosevelt. He was happy to be in the seat of power even if it were a situation of countervailing power in which his actions were checked. While delighting in his virtuosity he practiced a strong but flexible leadership.

Roosevelt's relations with legislative leaders were permanently tense. Whenever he could, he tried to cooperate, persuade, flatter, and cajole. But, they knew that he would proceed independently in matters in which he felt he could prevail because his political support was greater than theirs. He had an intimate knowledge of legislative moods and personalities, and his letters to members of Congress reflect his many attempts to influence them in terms of their perspectives.

However, his primary strategy of leadership was to put a backlash of public opinion on Congress in behalf of reform legislation. Over and over again in his letters, he wrote that he would not press for Congressional action on a given measure because it was not the kind of measure that had high public visibility and he was sure to lose. His letters to private citizens are full of soundings taken of public moods. He corresponded with opinion leaders and newspaper editors in all sections of the country as an intelligence device. Similarly, he often created public opinion. For example, when he wanted to make game wardens out of California forest rangers he wrote a California official and asked him to start a petition asking for this action so that such an act would seem to respond to public sentiment. He wrote to the President of Columbia University and asked him to stir up opposition to a bill, for "If I am to veto it I must have something to go on." [23]

He sought to keep his ties strong with labor leaders and leading business figures. His letters are filled with conciliatory notes to Catholics and other religious groups. In fact, his correspondence is one of the best textbooks of political strategy in a pluralistic society.

All of this influenced his Congressional strategies because his

[23] Roosevelt, *Letters,* II, p. 959.

intelligence sources told him how much the traffic would bear on any given issue.

Roosevelt was a master of the tactical maneuver against Congressional opposition. He always tried to keep powerful committee chairmen slightly off balance for fear of what he would do next. For example, in 1906 he was trying to get a bill for federal inspection and control of the meat packing industry past a skeptical James Wadsworth, Chairman of the House Agriculture Committee. Roosevelt wrote Wadsworth referring to an unpublished report on the bad conditions in Chicago packing houses. To publish the report would damage United States meat exports and stock growers, he said, and he wanted to withhold it for a time, "provided I can get the needed legislation. . . . With the report published I believe it would be possible to get substantially the Senate provision above referred to enacted into law." [24] This was a subtle threat. Wadsworth pushed the bill through but tacked on harmful amendments, whereupon Roosevelt released the report in a message to Congress. He had to settle for a compromise from the conference committee because he saw, by careful soundings, that Wadsworth had the votes and he did not. But, if he had relied solely on rational persuasion, the results might have been even less.

In the same year while in search of two new battleships he wrote a flattering note to Senator Hale, Chairman of the Naval Affairs Committee. He could not stand Hale but in this note he said that he believed Hale to be the most influential man in the Senate.[25] Then he raised the issue of a war scare. The West Coast riots over Japanese immigration were not only internal problems, he said, but also "they may possibly bring about war with Japan." Then, he asked for the battleships to which Hale was opposed. His other letters reveal that he did not think war with Japan was a serious possibility in the immediate future.

Roosevelt's virtuosity came to full height in the passage of the Hepburn Act. We have seen how he mobilized public opinion but he also had to funnel the heat against Old Guard Congressional leaders. His first tactic was to raise a phony issue as a potential threat. He raised the specter of tariff revision before them. His letters to the leadership allude to the great popular pressure for tariff revision and he even consulted Speaker Cannon about a possible Presidential

[24] Roosevelt, *Letters*, V, p. 282.
[25] Roosevelt, *Letters*, V, p. 473.

message on the subject. His other letters reveal that he did not want tariff revision, thought it a political hornet's nest, and was using it as a lever against the leaders. It seems likely that Roosevelt, Cannon, and Aldrich struck a bargain that tariff revision would be held back if railroad legislation were let through. Cannon gave the Hepburn bill a clear track in the House, but by agreement with Aldrich it was passed so late in the Session that the Senate could not act. Roosevelt came back with a new tariff scare. The Panama Canal Commission dramatically announced a new policy of buying materials in the cheapest markets, whether American or not. This so worried Congressional leaders that they called on Secretary of War Taft, who eventually rescinded the order. But the point had been made; the Hepburn bill came up in the Senate.

Just before that fight began, the President had a discussion with Senator La Follette about the proper strategy. La Follette advised pushing for the strongest possible set of regulations even if this meant losing in Congress. This was La Follette's crusading style. But Roosevelt wanted a bill. He wanted to make a start and he hoped that other bills would come afterwards. It is perhaps likely that he also wanted a personal victory. He did not like to waste his virtuosity and professional reputation on crusades. He knew that he had to carry Senate Republican moderates with him. They stood between progressives of both parties and the Old Guard. Thus, he had to push for a moderate measure.

Aldrich sought to outmaneuver T. R. by giving floor leadership of the bill to Ben Tillman of South Carolina, a Democrat, and a personal enemy of Roosevelt's. The President joined with Tillman behind a stronger bill to be passed by votes of progressives in both parties. When this failed because of a lack of votes, he easily switched back to his original plan, and, in alliance with Republican moderates, and one of their own as leader, he drove the bill through with moderate and progressive support. He had demonstrated where the only possible majority lay. He allowed an ambiguity to remain in the bill about the scope of judicial review over rate regulation because Senate uncertainty was very great on this point. He had won the Republican moderates and considerable Democratic support. He even forced Aldrich to climb on the bandwagon.

If Roosevelt had not been able to display such a diversity of styles the bill might not have passed. He carried the fight to the public. He showed tactical skill in his tariff feint and his handling of Tillman.

He understood the thinking of Republican moderates and played up to it. He knew all the keys on the piano and how to play them. He could amass more resources than Aldrich or Cannon.

Roosevelt's legislative achievements were a product of his empathy for public moods and his ability to articulate and dramatize them, as well as his sense of timing and his tactical skill. The Hepburn Act, the Pure Food and Drug Act, the Meat Inspection Amendment, the Employers Liability Act, the creation of the Department of Commerce and Labor, and conservation programs were major achievements. While these were not the achievements of a crisis President they were those of a President who understood the widespread desire for moderate reform and knew how to push hard for it.

T. R. had an open war with Congress during the winter of 1908–09 before he left office. He described it to his son in early 1909:

> I have a very strong feeling that it is a President's duty to get on with Congress if he possibly can, and that it is a reflection upon him if he and Congress come to a complete break. This session, however, they felt that it was safe utterly to disregard me because I made up my mind that it was just a case where the exception to the rule applied and that if I did not fight and fight hard, I should be put in a contemptible position; while inasmuch as I was going out on the fourth of March I did not have to pay heed to our ability to cooperate in the future. The result has, I think, justified my wisdom. I have come out ahead so far, and I have been full President right up to the end—which hardly any other President ever has been.[26]

He wanted to go out as a strong President who could dominate the scene to the end, and perhaps he felt an intuitive appreciation that the progressive movement was about to come to a head and was in search of a leader. Roosevelt, at all times a forceful leader, might have been even more forceful in the Presidency had he been in office at a time of great national reform. As it was, he had to be cautious and pragmatic, but seldom has Washington seen a more vociferous pragmatist.

Administrative Leader

William Howard Taft once complained to his brother that when he was in Roosevelt's Cabinet, T. R. had kept the federal administration in a state of turmoil by his habit of ignoring channels and intervening in administration at whatever level he pleased without notifying

Cabinet officers. This was written in a moment of pique with Roosevelt, but it reflects a truth. T. R. was a vigorous executive who was more concerned with an effective administrative process than with precise allocations of bureaucratic responsibility. In all of the administrative posts he held he had a temperamental impatience with red tape, bureaucratic obstruction, and restraints on his own authority. He was a hard worker with great energy and it was congenial to him to impress his personality upon everything he did. Therefore, he was an active, catalytic administrator. He sought to keep information coming up and coming in from the outside and to break the crust of administrative ossification by personally intervening at all levels. Furthermore, he loved to make decisions.

He was not at all the kind of compulsive personality who could not delegate authority. Roosevelt liked to have strong men under him and to delegate considerable authority to them. In his cabinet were a few strong able men, like Taft and Elihu Root, his Secretary of State, and he delegated much responsibility to them. However, it was not necessarily responsibility for the running of their own departments. Taft was really Roosevelt's personal agent, whom he used for political assignments, diplomatic missions, and specific administrative missions. Roosevelt ran the army himself, often acting over Taft's head and without Taft's knowledge, and the major decisions in the building of the Panama Canal were handled by the President, often over the head of Taft, who was nominally responsible. While John Hay was Secretary of State, Roosevelt handled the major diplomatic questions himself, often without Hay's knowledge. However, Root was a much stronger man than Hay and he was not afraid to stand up to Roosevelt. The result was constructive friction. As T. R. later said, "He fought me every inch of the way and together we got somewhere." [27] Much foreign policy was delegated to Root. However, it is fair to conclude that it was not in Roosevelt's nature to permit anyone else to make the great decisions of state, and that he regarded the administration as his government and Cabinet members as his agents. He would delegate authority or responsibility so long as this concept was not challenged.

This spirit was summed up in the following Rooseveltism in regard to sending the fleet around the world:

I determined the move without consulting the Cabinet, precisely as I took Panama without consulting the Cabinet. A council of war never

[27] Harbaugh, *Power and Responsibility*, p. 285.

fights, and in a crisis the duty of a leader is to lead and not to take refuge behind the generally timid wisdom of a multitude of councilors.[28]

Roosevelt took the position toward administration beneath him that he took in regard to influencing other actors in the legislative process. His success would ultimately depend upon his drive and skill. He wrote to his son Kermit in 1907:

> New difficulties have come up in connection with Panama. The truth is that I have a great number of tasks to do, and that except in a very few of them, either the best men I can get have weak streaks in them, or the conditions under which I work are so faulty that to accomplish even a moderate amount of good is exceedingly difficult. In other words the great majority of the instruments with which I work have each some big flaw. I have to endeavor to bear down as lightly as possible on the flaw and get the best results I can in spite of it; and when the instrument finally breaks, grin and pick up another one, probably no better and work as long as I can with it in its turn.[29]

T. R. had great concern for orderly administration. He was continually shaking up and reorganizing departments that functioned poorly, and he always insisted that organization be geared for action. He never tried to run the routine of any department, but he liked personally to intervene at any point in the administrative chain in order to get information or propel action. Just as he kept up a large correspondence with people outside the government as a kind of intelligence network to inform himself, so did he keep up a correspondence with many government officials of subcabinet level. Often, he implemented his policies through these men rather than through Cabinet officers. He corresponded with military officers over the heads of his secretaries. He wrote directly to officials of the Interior Department in the field. He even asked citizens in private life to check on the effectiveness of government employees in their areas.

He asked journalists to investigate government programs for him. He wrote the secretary of the A.F.L. and asked him to report directly to him any violations of the eight-hour day, which he would then turn over to the Labor Bureau for investigation.

He kept up a running correspondence with the "young Turks" in the navy about modernization matters, often on questions of detail. Roosevelt understood that a political administrator must immerse himself in the details of administration in order to keep control. His letters reflect this knowledge of detail, whether the matter was pointing

[28] Theodore Roosevelt, *Autobiography* (New York: The Macmillan Company, 1913), p. 592.
[29] Roosevelt, *Letters*, V, p. 589.

guns or fish hatcheries. But, he seldom allowed himself to become immersed in details. He simply sampled.

Of course Roosevelt's bureaucracy was tiny compared to that of today, and he did not have pressing problems developing from all sides as do Presidents today. Therefore, he could afford the luxury of personal intervention and detailed knowledge at all levels. But, it is very likely that were he President today he would find ways to ensure his control of executive bureaus. He would still intervene selectively and personally. He would ensure himself of more than one pipeline of information for making decisions. He would bring his restless vitality to administration. His specific methods would have been tailored to the times, but a man like T. R. could not have been a passive administrator. His drives, his beliefs, his talents, and his fascination with and virtuosity at the process of managing precluded this.

Post-Presidential Years

This is not the appropriate place to tell the story of 1912 and Roosevelt's smashing of the Republican Party in his bid for the Presidency. Roosevelt, the Bull Moose, is cast in popular history as the idealist who returned to political life in order to save the Republican party from its reactionaries and the betrayal of his principles at the hands of the conservative Taft, the man whom T. R. had mistakenly made his successor. Historians are convinced that this is only half the story. Taft was more conservative than Roosevelt. But more importantly, he was politically inept, and he could not stop the widening breach in the party between the progressives and the Old Guard. The progressive movement had come to full force and Taft was not willing to lead it. Roosevelt was willing. He gradually permitted himself to be drawn back into politics and by 1912 he was in open opposition to Taft and seeking the Republican nomination himself. What followed was inevitable, a fight for the nomination that Taft won, and Roosevelt's candidacy on a separate ticket.

Elting Morison, the editor of Roosevelt's letters, and John Blum, Roosevelt's most perceptive biographer, conclude that Roosevelt's decision to run in 1912 was dictated more by personal need than public duty. As Blum puts it: "To himself he may have admitted, though he probably did not, that in 1912—as in 1904 when he conquered and in 1908 when he painfully withdrew—he wanted desperately to be President." [30] Morison weighs the reasons Roosevelt

[30] Blum, *Roosevelt,* p. 147.

gave for his decision: Taft's ineptitude, the rise of progressivism, Roosevelt's advanced thinking on social and economic questions, and concludes that by themselves the reasons were not sufficient to explain his actions. Prudence would have dictated that T. R. wait until 1916 when he would have a clear field for the nomination. Morison sees Roosevelt's tragedy as coming home from Africa to turbulent times with nothing to do except sit at Sagamore Hill. His decision to retire in 1908 "must be taken as a moving act of the will, but an act nevertheless against his own nature."

Thus the delicate balance, retained so nicely whenever Roosevelt was in office, between his desire to serve the state and the need to act and control was, in the days of idleness, thrown out of adjustment. In 1912 the most natural urge, frustrated, before it was satisfied, by the decision of 1908, forced itself forward to spend, in one of his favorite phrases, and be utterly spent. The decision, in other words, when all the modifying circumstances are stripped away, was not so much required by the public as by a private welfare.[31]

Supporting evidence for this theory is seen in his conduct during World War I, when, frustrated by his lack of opportunity to play a central role, he became a ranting demagogue, consumed by his hatred of President Wilson. He angled for the Republican Presidential nomination in 1916 but he failed, and he was miserable to see another man President during an exciting war. He practically begged Wilson to let him command troops in France and he was denied this request.

Passage of the wartime draft act was delayed in Congress for two weeks while Senator Lodge, at Roosevelt's behest, amended it to authorize volunteer divisions of troops that would permit T. R. to lead troops in France.

His most disgraceful behavior was his demagoguery in behalf of one hundred percent "Americanism." Before large audiences he denounced hyphenate-Americans, called for the expunging of the German language from the schools, asked for loyalty oaths for teachers, said that conscientious objectors were in the enemy camp, equated labor unrest with Bolshevists and German Socialists, preached intolerance of all radicals and called for mass deportations, and, most importantly, preached the cult of war to the point where he turned many Americans against him. The public had always suspected that he had loved war too much, but now they were sure of it. The most charitable explanation of this behavior is that he was a frustrated

---

[31] Elting E. Morison, *Turmoil and Tradition* (Boston: Houghton Mifflin Company, 1960), p. 187.

man without outlets for his great talents who had virtually lost control of himself.

However, in the last months of his life, with the end of the war, he recovered his moderate posture and began to think of post-war domestic programs. His old progressive strain returned as well as his ambition. His letters and remarks made to friends indicate that he was hopeful the Republican party might nominate him for President in 1920. He died in 1919, but as he lay in his final illness he commented about his political enemies:

I don't mind having to die. I've had my good time. . . . and I don't mind having to pay for it. But to think that those swine will say that I'm out of the game.[32]

Conclusion

Roosevelt was the first modern President. He brought the office into the public view in unprecedented ways. He developed its potential as an agency of popular government. He pioneered in linking public opinion to legislative action. He was a politician who enlarged Presidential roles as a byproduct of his craftsmanship.

His search for drama and for power was at the root of his skill. His values reinforced this skill and gave him a sense of purpose. In the reversal of Lord Acton's dictum that "all power corrupts," we can say of T. R. that the possession of power restrained him. The tragedy of corruption took place in the years after his Presidency.

Roosevelt was thoroughly at home in the White House. To be President was to be himself. In the wedding of institution and personality, he set the pattern for Wilson and a later Roosevelt.

[32] Harbaugh, *Power and Responsibility,* p. 504.

CHAPTER 2

Woodrow Wilson:
The Moralizing Leader

IN HIS EARLY WRITINGS as a political scientist Wilson underestimated the potentialities of the Presidency as an agency for political leadership. As an admirer of the British parliamentary system he thought in terms of converting the American system into a parliamentary one in which the speaker of the house would be analogous to prime minister. In the 1880's when he first wrote, the Presidency was certainly underdeveloped. However, Theodore Roosevelt changed everything and Wilson's later writings, published when Roosevelt was in the White House, picture the President as the center of leadership in American government.

Wilson's contribution to the office was to institutionalize the President as legislative leader. At the height of his power he achieved a near fusion of executive and legislative powers in his own person. He showed what a President has to do to play such a role. His failures also indicated the possibilities of Congressional revenge and the impermanence of forceful executive leadership of Congress.

Wilson went even further than Roosevelt in using the office as a place of moral leadership. He did not innovate but he developed this role. His articulation of the New Freedom in terms of historic American ideals and his vision of a League of Nations and a world without war were his great achievements.

The imperatives of Wilson's personality led him into politics and accounted in large part for his skill and success and the way he shaped Presidential roles. But there was another side to the coin. The same personal qualities that made him such an able leader were also, under certain conditions, the source of rigidities that caused him to bring about his own defeat. There was a cyclical pattern to his career. As President of Princeton, Governor of New Jersey, and President of the United States he acted out a three-part drama: great achievement, overextension of his demands and deadlock with opponents, and final defeat. His career as President might have been forecast from the Princeton experience.

In each sphere of Presidential leadership his greatness was also his weakness. He could inspire visions but he tended to lose touch with the realities of public opinion. He could drive Congress hard but at times he could not moderate his pace. He dominated his administration but, at times, cut himself off from it by his jealousy of subordinates. These strengths and weaknesses were also rooted in his political personality.

Wilson picked up where Roosevelt had left off to set precedents for strong Presidential leadership. His flaws of personality did not weaken the Presidency as an institution but only himself and his policies. Unlike Roosevelt, his tragic flaw fully revealed itself in the White House. The fact that each of the Presidents of Action had a tragic flaw suggests that we cannot expect to find great political skill without such a flaw. The talent and the flaw seem to be rooted in the same political personality. However, the experience also indicates that the flaw hurts the person more than it does the institution.

Personality Needs

As a boy Wilson dreamed of growing up to become a great political leader. Taking Gladstone as his model, he practiced oratory in the pulpit of his father's empty church and in long walks through the woods. He placed particular importance on influencing others through the power of words. His ambition had a compulsive quality that was to appear often. One achievement had to be followed by another to allay a restless anxiety. He initially entered law as a path to a political career but found the practice of law so dreary that he entered Johns Hopkins to seek a doctorate in political science. This was a defeat in a sense because, so far as he could see, it meant an end to his hopes for a political career.

When his book, *Congressional Government,* was accepted for publication Wilson was at first elated, but this high point was followed by a depression revealing the restless drives at the root of his ambition. He wrote his fiance that ". . . success does not flush or elate me, except for the moment." The acceptance had pleased him "but it has sobered me a good deal too. The question is, what next? . . . I must push on: to linger would be fatal." [1] This drive to push on from a feeling of inner tension was to characterize Wilson's mature leadership. After the book was published and highly praised Wilson was

[1] Alexander L. George and Juliette L. George, *Woodrow Wilson and Colonel House, A Personality Study* (New York: The John Day Company, 1956), p. 23.

more sad than pleased and expressed it to his fiance, Ellen Axson, who had detected this mood:

> Yes . . . there is, and has long been, in my mind a "lurking sense of disappointment and loss, as if I had missed from my life something upon which both my gifts and inclinations gave me a claim"; I do feel a very real regret that I have been shut out from my heart's first—primary— ambition and purpose, which was, to take an active, if possible, a leading, part in public life, and strike out for myself, if I had the ability, a statesman's career. . . .
>
> I have a strong instinct of leadership, an unmistakably oratorical temperament, and the keenest possible delight in affairs; and it has required very constant and stringent schooling to content me with the sober methods of the scholar. . . .[2]

The next twenty-five years of academic life did not quiet this restlessness and unsatisfied ambition. He once tried to gain appointment as an assistant secretary of state, and wrote of his "old political longings thus set throbbing again." [3] As a professor at Princeton his books were famous, his lectures popular, and he was a leader among the faculty. Still, he was dissatisfied. He could not shake his desire for an active political life. He seems to have had the urge to leadership without any particular substance as the goal of action. This was the case throughout his career. His goals changed, but his desire to lead did not.

His frustrations caused him to live in a state of tension, to which he responded with a killing schedule of work. His family noticed an irritability that often seemed close to erupting. Then, in 1902 he was chosen President of Princeton and the frustration was over for a time. As he wrote of his appointment:

> It has settled my future for me and given me a sense of position and of definite, tangible tasks which takes the flutter and restlessness from my spirits.[4]

As he prepared his inaugural address he wrote his wife that he felt "like a new prime minister getting ready to address his constituents." [5] His old political longings had found an outlet.

[2] George, *Wilson and House,* p. 23.
[3] Arthur S. Link, *Wilson, The Road to the White House* (Princeton, N.J.: Princeton University Press, 1947), p. 38.
[4] Link, *The Road to the White House,* p. 21.
[5] John Morton Blum, *Woodrow Wilson and the Politics of Morality* (Boston: Little, Brown and Company, 1956), p. 22.

There was another side to Wilson's inner restlessness that was to appear in his style of leadership. All his life he sought relief from inner tension through the emotional support of uncritical, nurturing family and friends. All of his close friends had one thing in common: they were his uncritical admirers. As one friend wrote of him: "A person to obtain his intimacy, had to say very definitely 'I like you' or 'I love you'." [6] If a friend challenged his opinion in a serious matter, he broke off the friendship. This sensitivity to criticism was a great handicap to him as a leader.

Mental Traits

He once said: "It is not men that interest or disturb me primarily, it is ideas. Ideas live; men die." [7] However, he was seldom interested in ideas for their own sake but rather in how to put them to practical use. He was not intellectually versatile. He knew little of languages or literature and was indifferent to science, even to economics. He was primarily interested in ideas that related to his own ambitions to be a leader. He had a powerful, practical intellect, which was always in action, joining imagination and experience to practical solutions. He had a drive to reconstruct and order institutions, the Princeton eating clubs and the world of nations. His mind was very disciplined. Ray Stannard Baker wrote in 1916: "I have never talked with any other public man who gave me such an impression of being at every moment in complete command of his entire intellectual development." [8]

His study of history convinced him that great statesmen had the souls of poets and were thus able to articulate moral truths to multitudes. Therefore, Wilson often relied on his intuition as much, or more at times, than empirical data. He thought like a moralist rather than like a social scientist. It is interesting that he wrote *Congressional Government* in Baltimore without ever once going to Washington to see what he was writing about.

Values and Ideology

Calvinism was an important part of his makeup. The son of a Presbyterian minister, he was a devout man whose God was a thundering

[6] George, *Wilson and House*, p. 32.
[7] Link, *The Road to the White House*, p. 95.
[8] Link, *The Road to the White House*, p. 95.

Jehovah. To Wilson, God's moral judgements were absolute. Men were instruments of God's purposes. He joined this belief to his own throbbing ambition and sense of intellectual superiority and came to see himself as an agent of the Almighty God who had come to preach great truths to men. All of his life he had a feeling of special destiny. He told an aide after his election to the Presidency in 1912: "Remember that God ordained that I should be the next President of the United States." [9]

His weakness was that he tended to confuse his stubborn ideas with absolute moral law. Convinced that he was right, he was a poor compromiser, especially when he saw moral principles in a dispute. However, this rigid morality was also a strength because it sustained him through many bitter fights. He had a touch of predestination in his character, a certainty that his cause, the right cause, would ultimately triumph. This conviction often made it possible for him to cling to his principle no matter what the opposition was. It also permitted him to discard men when they ceased to be fit instruments for his purposes. He always subordinated men to causes.

During his academic years he was a Jeffersonian in his beliefs about the proper role of government. His values were those of nineteenth-century liberalism. However, when he ran for Governor of New Jersey he was converted to the progressive cause, in part out of electoral opportunism, in part out of a change of conviction. Certainly the theme of his New Freedom was Jeffersonian, that is, the use of government to regulate business to ensure competition and smallness and individualism against giant corporate monopoly. The content of this belief was sufficiently progressive to permit him to be a reform leader and sufficiently conservative to permit him to carry middle class opinion with him. What was more important for his style of leadership was his tendency to make absolute whatever he believed at the moment. At times this gave him great moral authority and at other times it made him too rigid. It was a byproduct of his Calvinism.

Certainly, his theory of leadership was not that of the trimmer, or compromiser, but of the moral teacher, who calls men to take account of their behavior in terms of great national ideals.

Wilson fashioned his political style during his Princeton presidency and a brief look at that experience will help us to draw his political personality more sharply.

[9] Arthur S. Link, *Wilson, The New Freedom* (Princeton, N.J.: Princeton University Press, 1956), p. 6.

President of Princeton

The time was ripe for reform at Princeton and in a burst of intense, creative leadership Wilson created a new curriculum, departmental reorganization, and introduced a modified tutorial teaching system. As Link puts it, "Never has so much life and vigor been injected at one stroke into an established university faculty." [10] Wilson was immensely popular with trustees, faculty, students, and alumni. His own persuasive enthusiasm swept all in his wake. However, in those first years no one challenged him or opposed his goals.

His first defeat came when, without warning, he secured trustee approval for abolition of the undergraduate eating clubs and their replacement by a system of residential quadrangles. When faculty opposition developed because of his method rather than his aim, he took his fight to the alumni in a series of intense speeches in which he made the plan a vote of confidence in himself. He lost the battle and for years could not bear to speak of it.

The quadrangle fight had intensified Wilson's rivalry with the Dean of the Graduate School, Andrew West. West, a tough and ambitious man, felt that Wilson had violated a promise to give the building of a graduate center priority over undergraduate housing. He presented a rivalry to Wilson that was intolerable. When West secured a gift from a wealthy donor for the construction of the graduate center, Wilson opposed it on the grounds of location. However, during a dramatic meeting of the board of trustees Wilson was confronted with the possibility of a compromise with West that would have met his terms, but he refused, revealing his personal antipathy. Eventually, after the donor withdrew his offer, Wilson attempted to have West removed as dean, and he raised a completely irrelevant issue of "democracy" at Princeton in connection with the fight, claiming that West wanted to segregate graduate students from the undergraduates. However, when a second donor appeared, Wilson was defeated. At this point he seized the opportunity to run for governor of New Jersey, and the trustees willingly accepted his resignation.

Wilson had turned a policy dispute into a personal fight. He had refused compromise because of pride and hatred. He had forecast a drama that was to be repeated almost exactly in 1919 in the fight between himself and Senator Lodge over Senate ratification of the League of Nations.

[10] Link, *Road to the White House*, p. 43.

At Princeton he developed his operating style of political leadership and also revealed its tragic flaws.

Political Personality

Did Wilson's very talents contain self-defeating forces? [11] Alexander George postulates that Wilson's driving ambition, his need for emotional support, and his inability to compromise in matters in which he had an emotional stake were consequences of childhood experiences. Wilson's father was a stern taskmaster who put the small boy through rigorous intellectual paces and often humiliated him in front of others in the process. George suggests that Wilson carried the scar of this experience for the rest of his life in the form of deep feelings of inadequacy. The search for power and fame was a form of compensatory striving to overcome these feelings. The refusal to compromise took place in situations that reminded him of his confrontations with his father, especially in emotionally-charged conflicts with rivals, West and later Senator Lodge. It was as if Wilson had resolved never again to bend his will to that of another.

This theory cannot be proven although it does make sense of much of Wilson's career. George suggests that Wilson's Calvinism was simply a cloak to cover his desire for power. He was morally correct and others must therefore accede to him. The same was true of his feeling of intellectual superiority. It is not necessary to go this far. Certainly, his Calvinism and the quality of his intellect reinforced his drive for power. They were all of a piece.

Wilson was not so rigid all the time or he could never have been a successful leader. He could be quite flexible in the pursuit of office and in strategies of leadership. His refusal to compromise occurred on matters in which he had so great an emotional investment that his whole identity was involved with victory, or in instances in which a deep personal rivalry was involved. It would be a mistake to picture Wilson as a neurotic or ill person. He was a very successful person who functioned quite well, but he did carry some kind of secret anxiety within him that drove him and which at times exploded.

Governor

Wilson took to political life easily and skillfully. As he himself put it: "This is what I was meant for, anyhow . . . this rough and tumble of the political arena. My instinct all turns that way." [12]

[11] See George, *Wilson and House*, Ch. 14, for a psychoanalytic explanation of Wilson's personality.
[12] Blum, *Politics of Morality*, p. 42.

Wilson's legislative leadership in his first year as Governor took the same pattern as his first years at Princeton. He drove a series of reform measures through the legislature by casting himself in the role of tribune of the people and arousing a potential public backlash against reluctant legislators. All of it had the fervor of a revival. He was the interpreter of the public will to those in his party in the legislature. As he said after he had won his fights:

> Everyone, the papers included, are saying that none of it could have been done, if it had not been for my influence and tact and hold upon the people. Be that as it may, the thing was done, and the result was as complete a victory as has ever been won, I venture to say, in the history of the country. I wrote the platform, I had the measures formulated to my mind, I kept the pressure of opinion constantly on the legislature and the programme was carried out to the last detail. . . .[13]

Wilson's chief weapon was the party caucus of the House Democratic majority. He broke percedent by personally attending these caucuses and argued for his program. In his first meeting he spent three hours pressing his case in dramtic language, appealing to moral principle and dropping threats that failure to comply with his wishes might require an appeal to the people by him and the subsequent defeat of the recalcitrant. He mostly appealed to their unselfish motives. One legislator gave his version of the first meeting:

> We all came out of that room with one conviction; that we had heard the most wonderful speech of our lives and that Governor Wilson was a great man. . . . opposition melted away under the Governor's influence.[14]

Wilson was riding on the capital of progressive agitation of the previous ten years, but, without his powerful leadership, his program could not have been enacted.

However, Wilson's second year as Governor was a legislative failure, and the failure reveals much about his political personality. In 1911 the Republicans won control of the legislature and Wilson refused to provide legislative leadership, even for the Democratic minority.

Link concludes that the failure of the 1912 legislative session was the result of Wilson's own personal limitations. He revealed his "temperamental inability to cooperate with men who were not willing to follow his lead completely." [15] This was a temperamental defect. He could not meet the situation of divided rule with a stance of patience,

---

[13] George, *Wilson and House*, p. 69.
[14] Link, *Road to the White House*, p. 255.
[15] Link, *Road to the White House*, p. 306.

negotiation, and compromise. So, he gave up leadership altogether. In this instance he did not care, because he already had his eyes fastened on the White House. Had it not been so, he might have engaged in a bloody fight with the legislature, reminiscent of Princeton.

Conception of the Presidency

In 1908 Wilson held this conception of the President:

> He can dominate his party by being spokesman for the real sentiment and purpose of the country, by giving direction to opinion, by giving the country at once the information and the statements of policy which will enable it to form its judgements alike of parties and of men. . . .
>
> Let him once win the admiration and confidence of the country, and no other single force can withstand him, no combination of forces will easily overpower him. His position takes the imagination of the country. He is the representative of no constituency, but of the whole people. When he speaks in his true character, he speaks for no special interest. If he rightly interpret the national thought and boldly insist upon it, he is irresistible; and the country never feels the zest of action so much as when its President is of such insight and calibre. . . . A President whom it trusts cannot only lead it, but form it to his own views.[16]

He always gave a parliamentary twist to his ideas on the Presidency and American government. He envisaged the President as a powerful prime minister, the leader of his party, who interpreted the popular will and led his party to implement it. He referred often to a basic axiom, the more power is divided, the more irresponsible it becomes. Thus, to him, individual congressmen represented parochial electorates and were not accountable to the nation at all, whereas he was the voice of the national will.

There was little, if any, room in this theory for legitimate congressional resistance to the Presidential will. To Wilson, the President was the leader of the party, and the party had a popular mandate and that was all there was to it. When he was convinced of the mandate and the morality of his policies, he was singularly unreceptive to compromise.

Notice that this is a theory of leadership at arms length. The President does not negotiate with Congress so much as he overpowers Congress. Likewise, the President deals with the public in an impersonal way, by using intuition to plumb their wishes and oratory

[16] Woodrow Wilson, *Constitutional Government in the United States* (New York: Columbia University Press, 1908), p. 68.

and writing to express them. This was the stiffness of Wilson's personality, to lead without bending his will to that of others.

Twice he thought of resigning and going to the country on issues of Congressional defiance of his requests.[17] He insisted on interpreting Congressional elections as personal plebiscites for or against himself. In short, Wilson saw a plebiscitary link between the President and the people. As a consequence, he was a strong leader when the tide for action was high but he was both temperamentally and intellectually unfit for leadership in a government of divided powers when the tide was running against him.

Leadership of Public Opinion

Wilson deliberately designed and developed a speaking and writing style that would move men and raise them out of parochial identities into the realm of great achievements. He came upon the stage of public life like a great moral prophet, preaching a "New Freedom," and caused many Americans to feel that the nation had been given a rebirth. His genius was to elevate particular issues into general principles, and this had a great appeal for pietist, moralist, Protestant, middle class America. Like Roosevelt, he had a gift for making phrases, for example, "the world must be made safe for democracy," "the war to end all wars."

His speeches appeared to appeal to reason, but in fact the appeal was quite emotional. He had a genius for spiritual generalities, repetition of ancient themes and symbols, and emotional heightening. All of his great achievements were cast by him in the language of American ideals. He used simple language with poetic power. He always appealed for support for measures in terms of principles that would be acceptable even to opponents of those measures. For example, his speeches in behalf of stronger anti-trust laws and lower tariffs used the language of free enterprise. The object of the legislation was to make the system, which of course all businessmen valued, work better in terms of basic principles. This refusal to attack or alienate any group and to appeal to opponents in terms of their own principles made it difficult to attack Wilson or his measures.[18] The legislative

---

[17] Wilfred E. Binkley, *President and Congress* (New York: Random House, 1962), p. 4.

[18] Marshall E. Dimock, "Wilson the Domestic Reformer," *The Philosophy and Policies of Woodrow Wilson,* ed. Earl Latham (Chicago: The University of Chicago Press, 1958), Ch. 15, p. 233.

program of the New Freedom was set in a frame of reference of Jeffersonian ideals, the protection of individuals from concentrations of power, competition rather than regulation, and the government as umpire rather than master. Each major piece of legislation was introduced after a thorough campaign of Presidential speeches in behalf of the principle behind the measure. Wilson understood that a leader cannot move beyond a position held by the great body of informed public opinion. However, once he found a clear moral principle on which to stand, he could preach to the people, and rally them. He brought to these visions the same powerful emotional drive seen in his bursts of creative leadership. His drive for power and his romantic notions of leadership came together.

There was a limitation in his method of persuasion. Like the evangelist who wants immediate and final conversion, the danger existed that Wilson might not convert his congregation permanently. He often confused his own inner fervor and sense of power with external response, assuming too readily that the one would automatically produce the other.

Wilson had a tendency to lapse into intuition in his interpretation of public opinion. He was especially prone to do this when he was swept up in a moral crusade of his own creation. He became so committed to it in his own mind that he assumed the public must have supported it as well. The tendency to replace empirical fact with intuition was inherent in Wilson's poetic conception of leadership.

Relations with the Press

He had an inability and an unwillingness to dramatize himself. He was incapable of doing what Theodore Roosevelt had done in using the press as a means for personal advertisement. Wilson concentrated on the intellectual and moral content of his messages to the nation, not on the techniques of publicity.

He understood intellectually the importance of a favorable press for the President, but he failed completely to establish good relationships with newsmen. On becoming President he initiated a biweekly news conference at which reporters might question him. This was intended as a release from the wearing individual conferences that he had disliked as Governor. Wilson did not like his Presidential press conferences and discontinued them as soon as the United States entered the war. In fact, he did not like reporters. He was shy and reserved by nature. Never, in his career, did he submit to interrogation and challenge without disliking it. As an intellectual he valued intellectual precision and abhorred the distortions and oversimplifications of the popular press. He valued his privacy and that of his family and never could understand that he and they were news in their own persons. He did not understand the new journalism that sought stories about personalities, and he could not use it for his own purposes. He wanted the press to transmit his words to the public intact, emphasizing their intellectual content.

He soon found a way to bypass the working press by reviving the direct Presidential address to Congress. In the Congressional forum his speeches would be reported without distortion or slighting. This decision was in keeping with Wilson's confidence in his own oratory, in his preference for bowling over potential opponents by the power of words, in his desire to set up direct ties with public opinion. It was a method congenial to Wilson's personality and in this sense was a necessity as well as a strategy. He spoke to Congress twelve times in his first term and ten times in his second term. Contemporary observers were agreed that these appearances were most effective in bringing national attention and support for Wilson's policies and administration.[19]

When the United States entered the war, Wilson appointed the Creel Committee on Public Information, which was a government agency of information and propaganda. Ray Stannard Baker, Wilson's official biographer, says that this idea grew out of Wilson's exasperation with reporters and the press. The committee's "Official Bulletin" gave the President an opportunity to bypass the working press altogether. He did not have to deal directly with media representatives or concern himself with public relations tactics. Creel took care of that. Wilson was left free to concentrate on the content of his public messages. It was all done at arms length.[20]

However, in this process Wilson so insulated himself from public opinion as to do himself great damage in the post-war period. Binkley thinks that the wartime hysteria of patriotism and hostility to dissenters to the war and critics of the President seriously misled Wilson into overestimating his hold on the public and may account for his ill-timed appeal for a Democratic Congress in 1918. Even though he had a warning of public disaffection in that election result, Wilson went to Paris convinced that he carried a popular mandate. In Paris, his inability to deal with reporters became a serious handicap to him. The Creel Committee no longer existed. He refused to see newsmen,

19 Cornwell, *Presidential Leadership,* pp. 46, 47.
20 Cornwell, *Presidential Leadership,* p. 55.

or to give out news, in Paris, with the result that he had no forum for the education of American public opinion as to his purposes. Opponents of the League had an advantage in those months to preach against the League, also, as post-war domestic problems increased the public became increasingly less interested in foreign policy. In Paris, he had no forum for expression, of the kind he liked. When he returned to America for his League fight, it was probably too late. The damage had been done. His dramatic Western speaking tour came too late.

Wilson's failure to educate public opinion in the League fight was perhaps both a strategic and a tactical one. He failed to develop a strategy because he was so caught up in his own private vision as to overestimate the degree to which the public supported that vision. And, he failed in a tactical sense simply because of his inability to use the working press as a means of transmission to the public. Both of these failures were the obverse of his great skills as a leader of public opinion. He was more prophet than manipulator.

Legislative Leader

After his first victory over Congress, as he was signing the bill into law, Wilson was heard to say: "I have had the accomplishment of something like this at heart ever since I was a boy." Yet, in a letter to a friend at the same time, he confided: "I am so constituted that I never have a sense of triumph." [21] Here we have an insight into the private drives behind public achievements.

However, there were public reasons as well for Wilson's legislative drive during his first term. He was elected on the crest of the progressive movement and knew the country was ripe for a reform leadership.

Wilson carried in a large Democratic Congressional majority that was relatively easy for him to direct because they identified their political futures with his success and thirsted for the patronage he had to dispense. He was a fresh personality, new to national politics and generally respected as a selfless man.

Once all of this is said, it is still true that Wilson was superbly fitted for his task. His drive, moral fervor, preaching, and understanding of the nature of Presidential power were the principal vehicles of action in the legislative program of the New Freedom.

[21] Blum, *Politics of Morality,* p. 71.

His legislative innovations seem commonplace today since all Presidents are, by common consent, legislative leaders. But, he was the first President to address Congress since Jefferson. When he went to Capitol Hill to confer with the leadership on pending bills, he revived a wartime practice of Lincoln's. For a time he fused the executive and legislative powers in his own person. He made Congressional leaders and committee chairmen his associates. This was consistent with his theory of the President as a party leader and with his compulsive drive to dominate. He brought legislative and Cabinet leaders together in meetings at which he presided. He mediated disputes within his Congressional party and, when necessary, used patronage offers and threats to get his way against recalcitrants. He relied primarily on Democratic caucuses in each house to produce party discipline in favor of his programs. It is difficult to recapture the effect that Wilson's personality had on members of Congress, but, evidently, his almost irresistible power of persuasion was his major asset as a legislative leader.

One congressman described a meeting with the President in which Wilson gave the impression "that we are all—President, Congress, and people—in the presence of an irresistible situation." [22] He did not see himself as a dictator. He wrote a friend that in leading Congress he was attempting to "mediate their own thoughts and purposes. . . . They are using me; I am not driving them." [23] However, at the same time, he wrote that he could not understand why members of Congress could not see their duty in a particular matter.[24] Once he saw his duty the opposition of others became illegitimate. Quite often he simply told those who opposed him that they were "wrong." All of it had the tone of a man who had little emotional or intellectual tolerance for those who disagreed with him. Wilson's style of leadership was not just a strategy calculated to fit the political situation; it was that and more. He had the opportunity to exercise his drive to dominate and there were, for a time, few checks on his imperiousness.

His first legislative fight was for downward tariff revision and in that fight he created a reputation for skill with Congress that gave him an advantage in subsequent fights. Calling Congress into special session he personally addressed a joint session and assumed a posture of command. Given the many interests opposed to a lower tariff as

[22] Link, *The New Freedom*, p. 154.
[23] Link, *The New Freedom*, p. 156.
[24] George, *Wilson and House*, p. 151.

well as Congressional reluctance to act, a weaker President might have floundered. Wilson won by refusing to compromise, threatening a veto, going to the Hill to direct the fight, working closely with Democratic Congressional leaders, and openly denouncing lobbyists who opposed features of the bill.

He then turned to a fight for banking and currency reform. Public opinion was anxious for action but fearful of radical departures. He quickly struck a compromise that would reconcile the demand of Southern and Western progressives for a decentralization of the banking system, away from Wall Street, with the need for centralized, government control. It was a system of regional banks presided over by a federal reserve board. He imposed this compromise on warring elements within his camp and forced them to take it on his terms. He presented the bill to House Democratic members of the Banking and Currency committee in a personal appearance at which he vowed that he would personally lead the fight. His comment in his diary at the time reflects his style of leadership:

> Not an hour can I let it out of my mind. Everybody must be seen; every right means must be used to direct the thought and purpose of those who are to deal with it and of those who, outside of Washington, are to criticize it and form public opinion about it. It is not like the tariff about which opinion has been definitely forming long years through.[25]

Again he appeared before a joint session. Financial leaders were already attacking the bill, and Wilson sought to keep his momentum going. When radical Democratic members of the House committee revolted and threatened to kill the bill, Wilson took over from Carter Glass, the Chairman, and by a process of persuasion and threat and pressure kept the rebels in line. He publicly blasted the large bankers after their organization attacked him, and this and the intervention of Secretary of State William Jennings Bryan with House radicals, who thought the bill too weak, caused House approval. In the key Senate committee, Wilson was confronted with three Democratic rebels, whom he threatened to attack openly in their own states on a speaking tour and then won them over by holding out and refusing compromise. Wilson won by gambling that the desire for action was so strong that he could have it on his terms.

In 1914 he pushed anti-trust legislation through Congress, and

[25] Link, *The New Freedom,* p. 214.

secured the creation of a Federal Trade Commission in much the same way. He drew up the bills in conference with the leadership, and forced the House Democratic caucus to approve them. Almost everyone wanted legislation and he was able to dominate by refusing support to measures he did not like. As long as he kept the initiative, and refused to compromise, the general atmosphere in favor of reform made him irresistible. His habitual tactic was to make a public refusal to compromise on the essential points of a measure. This served his opponents warning that he would not give in. So long as the tide was running with him this tactic worked.

In 1916, for reasons of electoral strategy as well as conviction, Wilson pushed a second series of reform measures through Congress: farm loan banks, workmen's compensation, a child labor law, and an eight-hour day for railroad workers.

During this brilliant first term there were premonitions of the failures of the second term. At times he showed himself to be a poor loser, revealing the deep emotional roots of his drive to dominate. When one of his appointments to the Federal Reserve Board was challenged in Congress, the President, in a letter to a congressman, falsified the nominee's relation with the International Harvester Company, which was the bone of contention. When the Senate Banking Committee voted against the nomination, Wilson conceded defeat privately but vented his feelings in a public letter of abuse against his Congressional critics.

When Congress defeated his 1914 plan for a government owned and operated shipping line, Wilson was so furious that he wrote a long, bitter indictment of the senators who had opposed him. Fortunately, it was not published. His old habit of turning policy disputes into personal quarrels was still with him.

The key to Wilson's success as a legislative leader was his ability to inspire men by visions. The whole country, including Congress, was swept in his wake. This had been his method in his Princeton reforms. He showed what a President could achieve if he could match the ability to lead public opinion with a rising demand for reform. He knew how to make Presidential power move with the "grain of history." However, just as his ability to paint visions sometimes cut him off from public opinion, so did his legislative drive sometimes lose touch with reality. Carried along by his own momentum, he could not moderate his course. We shall see this when we look at the fight for Senate approval of the League of Nations, the finale of his career.

Administrative Leader

Wilson's relationships with his unofficial adviser, Edward M. House, and his Secretary of State, Robert Lansing, tell much about Wilson as an administrator. House, who sought personal influence rather than public fame, made himself politically useful to Wilson by his astute advice. It was he who selected the first Wilson Cabinet. After 1914 he was the President's chief adviser and emissary on foreign affairs. Wilson trusted him completely and made him his friend and confidant. The key to this relationship seems to have been House's understanding of Wilson's need for praise, reassurance, and devotion. An excerpt from House's diary points this up: "[When the President asks for suggestions on drafts of speeches] I nearly always praise at first in order to strengthen the President's confidence in himself, which, strangely enough, is often lacking." [26] House understood that he could keep his influence only by keeping in the background and not appearing as a threat to the President. He was very careful to tell Wilson what a great man he was, to criticize only by subtle indirection, after first praising, and to convince him that he cared only to serve selflessly. For this reason, he refused an official post until his better judgment gave way and he accepted an appointment to the Paris Peace Conference Delegation. The eventual result was a rift between the two men that deprived Wilson of House's advice during the fight with the Senate over the League. Wilson began to suspect that House, as a delegate, was pursuing his own policies and not Wilson's and this was shattering to the President.

Lansing was superbly trained and qualified to be Secretary of State but Wilson never really trusted him and tried as best he could to bypass him. Their minds were quite different, Lansing's being analytical and inductive, Wilson's being intuitive and idealistic. But the chief cause of Wilson's distrust was Lansing's refusal to give the kind of loyalty that Wilson demanded. This meant intellectual submission and agreement as well as understanding, and Lansing was not the man for this. In a similar vein, Walter Hines Page, Wilson's Ambassor to Great Britain, was a friend and adviser so long as his reports contained what Wilson wanted to hear. But Wilson turned against him when he began to offer unsolicited advice and to criticize and report matters that displeased Wilson.[27]

[26] George, *Wilson and House*, p. 113.
[27] Link, "Wilson the Diplomatist," in *The Philosophy and Policies of Woodrow Wilson*, Ch. 9, p. 162.

Wilson's administrative style was much like that of Roosevelt in conception and purpose. He was determined to keep the essential decisions in the President's hands. To this end he refused to build up a White House staff, bypassed Cabinet officials on important matters, ignored channels and sent private emissaries on diplomatic trips, and so forth. However, his temperamental flaws were such that he often failed in the execution of this design. He was too fearful of delegation and tried to do too much himself.

Every male contact was seen by him as a potential contest of wills, which he must win. Therefore, he was usually on his guard against his own closest associates. He was set apart in a kind of loneliness. This had its strength in that he kept an autonomy and was never completely dependent on anyone. However, his great weakness was that he tended to shut himself off from advice. He was unable to accept it on matters in which he had a great emotional investment. The result was that, on occasion, he acted primarily out of his lofty moral intuition.[28]

Wilson viewed his Cabinet heads as departmental administrators and was willing to delegate a great deal of authority to them. In matters in which he had a personal interest he would let them do little. In matters in which he had no interest, he would let them do everything. Wilson especially dominated foreign policy and delegated authority for domestic policy. This meant that large areas of domestic policy were not coordinated within the Cabinet. He admitted that at times he lost track of what his department heads were doing. He had a tendency to become absorbed in important matters, to make them tests of his success as a leader, and to ignore all else. His fault was that he did not delegate authority in a way that permitted him to retain supervision over it. He just ignored many problems.

During much of his administration Wilson was absorbed in foreign policy decisions and his methods of making and carrying out foreign policy were a handicap to him. Link attributes them, in large part, to "his egotism, secretiveness, and urge to dominance." [29] Wilson believed that the President alone must make and control foreign policy, governed only by public opinion and his own conscience. Thus, he often ignored expert advice when it challenged his own intiuitive sense. House noticed Wilson's tendency in this direction and cited it as a "temperamental" defect.[30] After war broke out in Europe he noted

[28] Richard F. Fenno, Jr., *The President's Cabinet: An Analysis in the Period from Wilson to Eisenhower* (Cambridge: Harvard University Press, 1959), p. 56.

[29] Link, *The New Freedom*, p. 279.

[30] George, *Wilson and House*, p. 183.

that Wilson had a "one-track mind" that could not cope with both domestic and foreign problems at once. In 1916 he noted Wilson's inability to organize his work effectively:

> No one can see him to explain matters or get his advice. . . .
> The President does not know what is going on in any of the departments. . . . The President is not a man of action and seems incapable of delegating work to others.[31]

Wilson had one way of making decisions. First, he gathered all the facts. At this stage he was receptive to advice, although he seldom reached out for it. But he did want to listen to all sides of an argument. Then, he reached his decision by himself "after lengthy, painstaking, and solitary deliberation." [32] Once an opinion was formed in his mind, it became a moral position for him, and those who opposed him were either ignorant or immoral or both. In this way Wilson's Calvinism reinforced his need to dominate. He often equated loyalty with agreement and welcomed flattery instead of critical advice, with the result that his advisers often feared to tell him what they thought to be the truth. Few could handle him as cleverly as House.

Wilson did not work at opening up contacts with the world. White House appointments were usually brief, and during them Wilson listened and did not press his point of view. His physical energy was limited, but so was his patience. He did not savor contact with all kinds of men and thought most men fools and himself superior in knowledge and insight.

During the last stages of the war he increasingly isolated himself from his own government and concentrated his energies on visions for the future. He began to think of the verdict of history and to ignore certain practical political difficulties that were emerging. This failure was to come to light in the fight for the League of Nations.

The Fight for the League

Wilson's agony during the period of neutrality had been genuine and painful. He could not bring himself to lead America into the war on grounds of national interest alone. There had to be a higher moral cause. Once a cause was found, the war to end all wars and make the world safe for democracy became a burning crusade for him. He looked to the future and cast a messianic dream of a league of demo-

---

[31] George, *Wilson and House*, p. 188.
[32] Fenno, *The President's Cabinet*, p. 38.

cratic nations in a peaceful world. He had an opportunity to write a constitution for the world and his single-track mind focused on this goal and ignored the many practical obstacles to its realization. He developed an intolerance for those who challenged his vision, and he began to see himself as the agent of God and of the masses of mankind. He presumed that all men held to his ideals and that leaders who challenged him would be easily beaten.

In this, his greatest commitment, he failed to sense his growing isolation from the American people, from Congress, and from the Allies. He did not take the warning of the 1918 Congressional election defeat. In November, 1918, it became clear that Wilson could expect a fight with the Senate over ratification of the peace treaty, including the League of Nations. Congress was waiting to strike at the President. Resentment had been building up at his domineering reform leadership and at Wilson as the war dictator. During the war he had bullied Congress. Patriotism had restrained his opponents, but with the war's end, a fight was inevitable.

Historians agree that Wilson blundered in his fight with the Senate and finally killed his own idea of the League. It was the fight with West over again. He translated a substantive fight into a personal one and so structured the situation that he would have to lose unless his opponents would bend their wills to him completely. His first error was in not choosing prominent Republicans for the American peace delegation. He had never been able to work well with men of the same stature as himself, and he saw this mission as peculiarily his own. He also saw the conduct of foreign relations as the sole responsibility of the President.

It became apparent that he intended to bypass the Senate as much as possible. He did not keep it informed of the Paris proceedings. He said publicly that the Senate would find it hard to alter the treaty, thus making compromise hard for himself if it became necessary. This was his old strategy, which had worked so often.

Midway in the peace conference Wilson returned home to face growing Senate Republican opposition to the League of Nations. The majority of Republicans were "mild reservationists." Wilson might have brought them into his camp with modest compromises but instead he attacked all reservationists in a scatching speech.

There was a two-thirds majority in the Senate for American participation in a League, if mild reservations could be attached to the treaty, thus making it clear that American sovereignty was not threatened by participation. He would not compromise. He saw the issue as both personal and moral and he never negotiated this kind of an issue.

Senator Lodge opposed an American role in the League but knew that the only way to prevent it was to get Wilson to defeat himself. He based his strategy on his evaluation of Wilson's personality. Knowing that Wilson hated him he judged that Wilson would never agree to amendments inspired by Lodge. Wilson was not detached enough to see Lodge's game. Historians are agreed that the mild reservations were not harmful to the League, but through the summer of 1919 Wilson refused compromise. When warned that the treaty could not pass unamended, he said, "Anyone who opposes me in that I'll crush." [33]

In September Wilson resolved to appeal directly to the people. His speeches on his Western tour condemned compromise and attacked all reservationists. He drove himself relentlessly, collapsed, and after his return to Washington suffered a stroke. The stroke did not injure his mind but his physical helplessness seems to have further prejudiced him against compromise. He wrote the Democratic floor leader, Senator Hitchcock, that no compromise was possible, and that he would veto such a treaty. This kept Senate Democrats behind Wilson. However, it put the mild reservationists behind Lodge and the Senate adopted Lodge's amendments. Wilson's hope was that the treaty as amended by Lodge would be defeated and that the original version would then pass.

The amended treaty was then defeated with Democratic votes. About eighty senators still wanted a League. Wilson again refused to compromise with the moderate Republicans. As in the fight with West, Wilson had lost sight of the substantive issue, and was engrossed in his hatred of Lodge. It was a personal fight, and it was less painful for Wilson to sacrifice his own treaty than it was to compromise. In March, 1920, enough Democratic senators voted again to defeat the treaty. Wilson had slain his own child.

Was Wilson acting in response to old inner conflicts that were inappropriate to the situation? We cannot know. He was acting in a way harmful to his own goals. His behavior was inappropriate in this sense.

Wilson's messianic vision and Calvinist moralism contributed to his rigidity, but it is hard to see how they could have shaped his tactics so forcefully. They were the engines of his moral commitment but often before he had been able to combine moral commitment with

---

[33] George, *Wilson and House*, p. 288.

tactical realism. In this fight something was triggered in Wilson that made it impossible for him to bend his will to that of others.

Conclusion

Like Roosevelt, Wilson's contributions to the Presidency were a function of his needs and drives. He played Presidential roles in the ways most congenial to his political personality. He was especially fitted to be a great legislative leader, a tribune of the people, in a period of popular reform.

It may be that he was capable of being an effective leader only in periods when the tides of public opinion were running with him. His very ability to inspire others suffered from his inability to see when the views of others were beginning to diverge from his own. His ability to drive a legislature to action suffered from the difficulty he had in slowing his own momentum and compromising. He was primarily a leader who could work well with one issue at a time and who might have had difficulty handling the multiple and simultaneous problems of today's Presidency.

CHAPTER 3

Franklin D. Roosevelt: The Manipulative Leader

FRANKLIN ROOSEVELT excelled at the two roles that T. R and Wilson had developed, public opinion and legislative leader. But his particular contribution to the Presidency was as an administrative leader. He was the first President to have to cope in peacetime with a giant federal bureaucracy, much of which was the result of his own New Deal. His search for control taught later Presidents about the problems they would have in getting information, coordination, control, and action out of bureaucracy. His sense of Presidential power, which was a function of his desire for personal power, served him well in this task and made him master in his own house.

He was a combination of the lion and the fox in his style of leadership in all three Presidential roles. At times he was a source of inspiration and courage. At other times he was cautious and calculating. In both instances he was responding to chords within his personality, the central theme of which was the enjoyment of charming, manipulating, and influencing others.

He made the Presidency a symbol of national strength and purpose in times of depression and war. He ensured that the President would always thereafter have to be chief legislator. Theodore Roosevelt and Wilson had initially developed these roles, each of them emphasizing one. F. D. R. was their pupil and he brought all three roles to fulfillment. Since his time, observers of the Presidency have called for the exercise of skill in all three roles. All subsequent Presidents have been judged by the standards of skill in each role that F. D. R. set. Often this is done unfairly because it is too easily forgotten that he was President in times favorable to strong, skillful leadership. Like T. R. and Wilson he moved with the "grain of history." Like them, his political personality gave him skill, but that skill was enhanced by his moral leadership.

Like T. R. and Wilson, his political personality had its darker side, and this showed itself occasionally during his tenure. However, the results were not as explosive as in the other two men because his inner imperatives were of a different quality. T. R. and Wilson needed power to allay deep anxieties. F. D. R. needed power as a fulfillment of his remarkable self-confidence. His particular flaw was that of egoistic self-confidence. At times his certainty that he could prevail over others simply by exercising his manipulative skills or turning on his charm led him to mistakenly ignore difficulties and obstacles. This flaw was grounded in his talent.

Personality Needs

Franklin Roosevelt grew up on the family estate in the Hudson River Valley in the nurture of loving parents, relatives, tutors, servants, and pets. He did not go to school until he was fourteen and the estate was his kingdom. An only child, he was the center of his mother's attention and she encouraged him to develop his personality and talents. He was a beautiful boy glowing with vitality whom everyone liked. He reciprocated this world of affection in his liking for and trust in others. He came to take it for granted that he should be the center of attention, and thus as a boy he began to develop those skills that would bring him attention and approval.

He began to develop the skills of the politician at Groton and Harvard. Entering Groton late, he was an outsider for a time, and he worked hard at winning the approval of the other boys. At Harvard he was faced with the same problem of an environment that was not immediately responsive to his demands. His response was to become a campus politician. He became editor of the Crimson and Marshal of his graduating class. As his biographer states: "The pleasure gained from the sport of maneuvering and manipulation, and the status that came with political prize, held strongest appeal for him. Unwittingly, in these pursuits he took the first stride toward becoming an effective politician." [1] He showed a talent for personal leadership. His co-editor remembered that "in his geniality was a kind of frictionless command." [2]

From his earliest years Roosevelt hid his thoughts and motives behind a mask of geniality and conformity. Years later his associates were to emphasize the mystery of the man, how he never fully revealed himself to anyone. Biographers are agreed that this mask was a protective cover for him in a social world in which he did not feel

[1] Frank Freidel, *Franklin D. Roosevelt, The Apprenticeship* (Boston: Little, Brown and Co., 1952), p. 73.
[2] Freidel, *The Apprenticeship,* p. 65.

completely at home. He expected more from his environment than it had given him. The practice of corporation law in New York City was not sufficient for fulfillment and at the age of twenty-eight he gravitated into a political career.

As one biographer said: "The design of his life is marked by a growing sense of the urgency of influencing those immediately surrounding him and of understanding their needs and desires." [3] Politics would give him an opportunity to like and be liked. It would also give him an opportunity to realize a vague but genuine idealism.

He announced to his fellow law clerks that he intended to pick good Democratic years and be, successively, a member of the New York legislature, Assistant Secretary of the Navy, Governor of New York, and then, with luck, President.

In the first good Democratic year, 1910, he went to the New York Senate. There, as had his cousin, he attracted attention as a foe of the worst elements of bossism in his own party.

At the age of thirty-one he became Assistant Secretary of the Navy under Woodrow Wilson. There he developed his knack for getting along with all sorts of people, naval officers, labor leaders, congressmen. He showed a style of straddling conflicting points of view and giving half a loaf to each, which was to be one of his characteristics as President. This trait was deeply rooted in his personality for in similar fashion he refused to mediate between his domineering mother and shy wife, and he simply accepted the situation. As Schlesinger says, he "preferred practical compromise to basic diagnosis." [4] He wanted to be on good terms with everyone and the result in the Navy Department was his great success as a diplomat among interests. The Secretary of War, Newton D. Baker, noticed how F. D. R. educated himself and commented:

Young Roosevelt is very promising, but I should think he'd wear himself out in the promiscuous and extended contacts he maintains with people. But as I have observed him, he seems to clarify his ideas and teach himself as he goes along by that very conversational method. [5]

Before he was forty, F. D. R. had had considerable political experience for such a young man, in the executive branch for seven years

---

[3] Edgar Eugene Robinson, *The Roosevelt Leadership, 1933–1945* (Philadelphia: J. B. Lippincott Company, 1955), p. 42.

[4] Arthur M. Schlesinger, Jr., *The Crisis of the Old Order* (Boston: Houghton Mifflin Company, 1957), p. 329.

[5] Frances Perkins, *The Roosevelt I Knew* (New York: The Viking Press, 1946), p. 21.

and as his party's candidate for Vice-President in 1920. The tragedy of polio in 1921 did not deter him from a political career but instead reinforced his ambition. There is general agreement that polio did not so much alter Roosevelt's personality as it reinforced certain traits that gave him new discipline. His fight only confirmed and strengthened the joyous optimism with which he had always faced life. He would not admit the possibility of failure and although there is evidence that he was terribly depressed at times, he radiated courage and cheer to those around him. This gave him a courage with which to meet later political crises, a certain serenity that all who later worked with him noticed. When asked in later years if things worried him-he would say, "If you had spent two years in bed trying to wiggle your big toes, after that anything else would seem easy." [6]

He achieved mental discipline. Having always been a restless worker, he was forced to develop his powers of concentration because he could not run from tasks. They were there in front of him. His wife felt that his self-control and power of patience were increased by the long, slow treatments. Certainly, this increased patience, and perhaps an increased detachment from flux that went with it, was of great help to him as a political strategist in later years. His sympathy for people and especially for the unfortunate was strengthened. He had always enjoyed people but after his illness, Schlesinger says:

> They were his vital links with life, and his extroverted Rooseveltian sociability was compounded by his invalid's compulsion to charm anyone who came to his bedside. He sought more intensely than ever to know people, to understand them, to win them to him. Sometimes he even blurred his own feelings in an excess of amiability . . .
>
> But the desire to be liked also opened him up to their needs and fears. It explained in great part the genius for assimilation within him which was developing and which was giving him so extraordinary a receptivity. Invisible antenna stretched out, picking up with faultless precision the intangibles of human emotion. The individual case was for him the center of the learning experience; from it, he extrapolated with bold confidence to the nation and the world. [7]

In the broadest sense of the word Roosevelt sought to win "attention" from others. One of his ambassadors once said, "If he thought that you didn't like him, he'd practically jump over a chair to get to you." [8] His charm was legendary and he courted and wooed people and relied on it as a political instrument.

[6] Schlesinger, *The Crisis of the Old Order,* p. 406.
[7] Schlesinger, *The Crisis of the Old Order,* p. 407.
[8] John Gunther, *Roosevelt in Retrospect* (New York: Harper and Row, 1950), p. 34.

He did not seem to suffer the psychological anxieties of the first Roosevelt and Wilson about popularity and approval. He began from a position of psychological strength. The world would naturally love him for himself, and he had a right to this love. If there was a pathology here it was not one of insecurity but of overconfidence.

Mental Traits

Roosevelt was highly intelligent but he was not an intellectual or did he place great stock on logic and abstract reason. He thought with his whole personality. He did not enjoy debate and argument based on the orderly presentation of conflicting cases. Frances Perkins put it this way:

> His emotions, his intuitive understanding, his imagination, his moral and traditional bias, his sense of right and wrong—all entered into his mind and unless these flowed freely through his mind as he considered a subject, he was unlikely to come to any clear conclusion or ever to a clear understanding.[9]

He made decisions by a process of gradual absorption of information from many different viewpoints. He always sought out concrete, human examples in understanding problems or the possible effects of policies. He had immense curiosity and a memory for detail and could bring to bear all of his wide experience on a problem.

His mind was not orderly. He could concentrate on several different things at once and he had an almost perverse love for combining opposite suggestions in a common solution. This often made political sense but it also reflected his preference for empathetic broker leadership. For example, during the 1937 fight over reform of the Supreme Court he wrote Henry Stimson that the "truth" was probably halfway between Stimson's "position on court packing and his own." [10] Because of his ability to reason with his whole personality he was able to see that in democracy the demands of consensus may take precedence over those of rationality and logic in the formulation of policy.

He was open-ended in his thinking, placing final reliance on no one idea or group of advisers. He had a lack of final commitment that gave him great flexibility in meeting new situations. But, because of his buoyant temperament, he never doubted that the answer could be found.

9 Perkins, *The Roosevelt I Knew,* p. 153.
10 Gunther, *Roosevelt in Retrospect,* p. 112.

Ideology

F. D. R. once told a reporter who asked him for his "philosophy" that he was "a Christian and a Democrat—that's all." [11] His wife wrote: "Throughout the whole of Franklin's career there never was any deviation from the original objective—to help make life better for the average man, woman and child." [12] This was the *noblesse oblige* of the aristocrat.

The old Dutch families of the Hudson River Valley were country squires who felt only contempt for the new and vulgar wealth of the great industrial and financial families. They also had a feeling of *noblesse oblige* for the common people who came within their orbit of obligations. These attitudes were reinforced in Roosevelt by the influence of the headmaster of Groton, Endicott Peabody. Peabody had studied in England and had been greatly influenced by Charles Kingsley and other Christian socialists and by the Tory democracy of Disraeli.[13] He preached this gospel of social responsibility to the Groton boys, and Roosevelt often in later years acknowledged his debt to these ideas. In addition, the influence of his distant cousin, his wife's Uncle Ted, was great on the young man. These influences, when joined to his temperament and mentality, created an ideology of operationalism in which the power of government was to be dedicated to human needs. But he was never a radical. He was a liberal with conservative roots, an ideal bridge between tradition and reform.

Political Personality

It is clear that Roosevelt's political personality was a unity. He was open-ended in his reaching out for attention and support and his genuine liking for people. He was open-ended mentally and ideologically, and in both his mental habits and ideals he sought to create ties of affection and support with people. The skills that he developed to influence and lead others reflected his political personality. He was an artist at interpersonal relations; he knew how to combine diverse advice in unified solutions and to strike chords of popular support by his affirmation of old ideals in new forms. At the root of it all was

[11] Perkins, *The Roosevelt I Knew,* p. 330.
[12] Eleanor Roosevelt, *This I Remember* (New York: Harper and Row, 1949), p. 67.
[13] Freidel, *The Apprenticeship,* p. 38.

the love of process, and himself at the center of process, as the master artist, the master politician, but a politician with a heart and a vision.

Governor

He functioned as though he had been Governor for years. He was able to give full scope to the techniques of public relations that more or less came naturally to him but which he had refined over the years. He knew how to give speeches a dramatic theme, for example, beginning a speech on water power with a textual admonition to the power companies, "Thou shall not steal." [14] His speeches were couched in everyday terms and concrete illustrations. He developed the technique of the radio "fireside chat," which permitted the warmth and color of his rich voice to enter the homes of citizens. On his trips around the state he made the people feel that he was deeply interested in their problems.

When the Republican-dominated legislature defied him and ignored his program, he took his case to the public in a series of speeches and tours. He was determined to dominate the legislative process and in the long run he was able to find issues that both Democratic and Republican voters could support and which he forced the Republican-controlled legislature to consider by his policy of publicity. His legislative success was due to his sense of direction about policy, his formulation of mildly progressive measures that were widely supported, his dramatic use of language, his determination to dominate, his love of the political game, and his sense of long-range strategy, by which he pulled the legislature into the trap of defying him and then forcing them to capitulate.

Conception of the Presidency

F. D. R. once asked a friend, "Wouldn't you be President if you could? Wouldn't anybody?" [15] His conception of the Presidency was himself in the White House.

. . . he saw the job of being president as being F. D. R. He wanted mastery, projected that desire on the office and fulfilled it with every sign of feeling he had come into his own. Self-confidence so based was bound to reinforce his sense of purpose and to guarantee reliance on his sense of power.[16]

---

[14] Samuel I. Rosenman, *Working with Roosevelt* (New York: Harper and Row, 1952), p. 23.
[15] Gunther, *Roosevelt in Retrospect,* p. 49.
[16] Neustadt, *Presidential Power,* p. 155.

Throughout his entire pre-Presidential career he had studied the techniques and purposes of Presidential power, and his two greatest teachers had been "Uncle Ted" and Wilson. He conceived, as they had, of the Presidency as a place of moral leadership and he understood that a sensitivity to personal power was essential for Presidential achievement. He wanted power for its own sake but he also wanted what it could achieve. He once said, "I want to be a preaching President—like my cousin." [17] This superb self-confidence and this sense of history were, when joined with technique, to be immense, however intangible, sources of Presidential power.

But if he was a lion he was also a fox. He was a lion during periods of crisis and national affirmation when he could be the symbol and voice of popular demands for action. In periods of lull or conflict he could be a fox who acted within the limits of what he thought the traffic would bear. In each case the skills were different but in both instances they were informed by a sense of Presidential power.

Leadership of Public Opinion

When he told the nation in his first inaugural address that it had nothing to fear but fear itself, he was speaking from his own experience and temperament as well as to the external crisis. In this fusion of man and situation and theme he struck a deep chord in the American character, which is optimistic and activist. He had a kind of personal elation and air of expectation about taking office that spread across the nation.

After Roosevelt died several people told John Gunther, "I never met him, but I feel as if I had lost my greatest friend." [18] Millions of Americans felt such a personal affection for him. His mail indicated that people saw him as a friend who cared personally about their problems. He gave this impression in his radio talks. His voice told people that he liked them and cared about them. Schlesinger sums it up:

It was the image of human warmth in a setting of dramatic national action which made people love him, not any special necromancy as a politician. Can the political art in any case be practiced apart from objectives? . . .

It was not any technical wizardry as a politician but rather his brilliant dramatization of politics as the medium for education and leadership

[17] Arthur M. Schlesinger, Jr., *The Coming of the New Deal* (Boston: Houghton Mifflin Company, 1959), p. 558.

[18] Gunther, *Roosevelt in Retrospect*, p. 4.

which accounted for his success. Beyond the backdrop of the depression and the deeds of the New Deal, Roosevelt gained his popular strength from that union of personality and public idealism which he joined so irresistibly to create so profoundly compelling a national image.[19]

Relations with the Press

F. D. R. once said that the Presidential press conference was "a special art all by itself." [20] He met the press twice a week in his office in a relationship of spontaneity and give and take, which both the President and reporters enjoyed immensely. He liked reporters and conveyed this regard to them by learning their first names, reading their stories, kidding with them, and inviting them to secret Sunday night suppers at the White House at which Mrs. Roosevelt cooked scrambled eggs. Most importantly, he understood that they would be grateful to a President who gave them news. In serving their self-interest he served his own. They responded to his warm personality and to his political skill, as well as to his New Deal policies, with the result that he received a good press in spite of the fact that the editorial pages opposed him overwhelmingly.[21]

He often made "background" comments in which a White House spokesman, but not the President, could be quoted. The New Deal was making many new policy departures and the working press and general reader needed education. Roosevelt provided it by his background explanations, which helped put policy in context. This was especially true of his "budget seminars" in which he went over each yearly budget with reporters.

He learned about public opinion from press conference questions. He was particularly skillful in the use of trial balloons and in judging the feedback of opinion.

He dominated his press conferences by his verbal agility. He turned questions to his own advantage, made sure that certain news items became the news of the day, and demonstrated his incredible knowledge of governmental details to the wonder of reporters. He used press conferences as a forum for discussion and selling of policy and as a means of projecting his personal image to the public. Speeches and radio talks were too infrequent for these purposes, but the biweekly press conference kept people interested in what he was doing and thus they created a general receptivity for more specific appeals.

[19] Schlesinger, *The Coming of the New Deal*, p. 573.
[20] Schlesinger, *The Coming of the New Deal*, p. 560.
[21] Cornwell, *Presidential Leadership*, Ch. 7, *passim*.

Fireside Chats

He used the radio as a means of direct communication with a national audience. The color and warmth of his voice and his facility of expression were perfect for broadcasting. He once told Orson Welles that they were the two best actors in America.[22] He worked hard on his "fireside chats." They were filled with the simple, direct, homey appeals and vivid analogies that he liked, for example, the justification of Lend Lease to Britain in terms of loaning a garden hose to a neighbor whose house was on fire. Frances Perkins watched him during his radio talks and noticed that he was not conscious of those in the room. He gestured and smiled as if the radio audience could see him and it was clear that he made an effort to visualize them listening in their homes. When she sat with people as they listened to his talks she noticed that they sensed that Roosevelt felt affection for them, and they responded in kind.[23]

He made his radio talks only two or three times a year, for fear of wearing out his welcome with the public. He felt that people tired of causes and leaders and therefore a President should not squander his capital but use it judiciously. He made most of his chats when Congress was away and timed them with his subtle estimate of likely public response. He seldom made specific requests but talked generally about administration achievements and plans and set events in context.

During the low period of his political support, from the fight over the Supreme Court to Pearl Harbor, his radio talks were less effective. He was on the defensive against Congress and the public was less eager for government reforms. He was at his best in times of crisis when he could affirm and inspire.

Teaching Public Opinion

Roosevelt saw his job as that of teaching public opinion. He felt this had to be done in terms and a frame of reference that the public could understand and that new ideas could not be unleashed all at once. He was not willing to take chances and declare himself in a final way on specific issues before he knew the state of public opinion. To go out on a limb, in his mind, was to risk undercutting his political resources. He always tried to pick his own issues and his own time and not let anyone, friend or foe, smoke him out. When he wanted

---

[22] Gunther, *Roosevelt in Retrospect,* p. 62.
[23] Perkins, *The Roosevelt I Knew,* p. 72.

to move in a new direction he would press gently and then watch public reaction through the many information channels he had built up. If the response was good, he moved another step, and so on, step by step, testing as he moved. If the response was bad, he withdrew and waited for a better time.

A classic example of his technique was his treatment of social security. He decided not to push for social security legislation in 1933, although he desired it, because he felt public opinion was not ready.[24] It seemed too alien to the American tradition of self-reliance. He first mentioned the subject in early 1934 at a press conference for business paper editors. This talk showed "his masterly skill at painting the issue in colors that would be most appealing to the audience at hand." [25]

He stressed the actuarial soundness of the idea, the fact of worker contributions, the limited government role, and so forth. From June, 1934 until January, 1935, when legislation was sent to Congress, he pursued an educational campaign, which he subtly tied to the November, 1934 Congressional election. He sent Congress a general message discussing social security objectives. He devoted two fireside chats to the subject, taking great pains to deny that social security was an alien, socialist idea. He set up a commission to study it. He went on tour and discussed it in several speeches. Then, in January, 1935 he discussed social security in his State of the Union message. After the proposal had gone to Capitol Hill, he mentioned it only once publicly before it passed in August. This was in an April fireside chat when he nudged a stalling Congress along. He mentioned it often in his press conferences but only as "background" so that he was not quoted directly. Thus, he did not appear to be pressuring Congress but he kept the issue alive.

This study shows Roosevelt's sense of sureness and touch in leading public opinion. His strategy was to convince moderates that social security was congenial to traditional American values.

Legislative Leader

F. D. R.'s first One Hundred Days in office brought forth a great burst of legislation: the Banking Act, Economy Bill, Securities Act, Farm Relief Act, Federal Relief Act, Railway Reorganization Act, and the creation of the N.R.A., A.A.A., C.C.C., and T.V.A.

What distinguished F. D. R. among national leaders was that he

---

[24] Cornwell, *Presidential Leadership,* Ch. 6, *passim.*
[25] Cornwell, *Presidential Leadership,* p. 123.

was not afraid to act. His sense of purpose enhanced his sense of power. The banking crisis was at its height. The large Democratic majority in Congress was willing to follow effective leadership. Roosevelt secured a hold on public opinion through his speeches that he never really lost.

He received the support of Congressional leaders of both parties. Often Democratic leaders did not know the content of legislation until it was introduced but they subordinated themselves to the President. His fights were with the representatives of interest groups in Congresss who sought to block or amend legislation in their favor, for example, veterans, agricultural processors, and farm groups.

He needed his great tactical skill to get his program through in the form he wished. In his inaugural address he implied to Congress that if it did not act to meet the emergency he would ask for special Presidential powers to act without it. He used patronage in the form of a carrot and stick by making no patronage appointments until the special session was over and the program passed. Congressmen were encouraged to support the White House on a *quid pro quo* basis. There was thus a "tinge of expectancy" in Roosevelt's relations with the legislators.[26]

He combined his sense of timing with an awareness of the needs of Congress. The Economy Bill met resistance because it cut veterans' pensions among other things. Roosevelt took the heat off by sending a request to Congress for softening of the prohibition laws at the same time. They could vote for legal beer and sneak the Economy Bill through, which they did.

He saw Congress as an arena in which national forces contended and he shaped his legislative movements to his larger formulations of strategy about the state of opinion in the country. As we saw with the enactment of social security, he liked to feel his way, balancing the imponderables of national life until such time as he felt a consensus had been created. No one saw the total strategy, only the pieces as they unfolded. He perhaps developed it himself without plan as he acted. His speech writers had to write about policy without knowing the strategic and tactical intent. His White House aides served him in the same unquestioning way. He was good at this because for years he had known how to conceal his thinking processes. His flexibility and secretiveness made him an elusive target for opponents and a hard man to block.

He carefully set up priorities of administration legislative requests. He knew that his political resources with Congress were limited, and

[26] Binkley, *President and Congress*, p. 301.

he would put his reputation on the line only for "must" legislation. Departments and agencies could push bills but he would personally support only a few.

Congress was made up of veterans to whom no President could dictate. Roosevelt's achievements were more amazing in light of the fact that most members of the Democratic leadership were not New Dealers. He chose to work through them rather than through the progressive rank and file. He wanted immediate legislative gains and gave little thought to the creation of an enduring progressive coalition in Congress. His success with Congressional leaders was a triumph of personal diplomacy. He dealt with them with such skill that often his personal role made the difference between defeat and passage of a bill.

Roosevelt's leadership talents lay in his ability to shift quickly and gracefully from persuasion to cajolery to flattery to intrigue to diplomacy to promises to horse-trading—or to concoct just that formula which his superb instincts for personal relations told him would bring around the most reluctant congressmen.[27]

This kind of manipulation of his own personality to win the acceptance of others was something he had been doing skillfully in private life since boyhood. When Congress was in session he spent three or four hours a day either on the telephone or in conference with members of Congress. He was "a master at the art of providing congressional gratification . . . the easy first name, cordial handshake— radiant smile—intimate joke—air of accessibility and concern—quasi-confidential interview—photo at White House desk—headline in home town paper." [28] He boasted to aides about his virtuosity in handling legislators. Once a visitor waiting in the anteroom outside the Presidential office saw F. D. R. just as he had succeeded in calming down an angry Congressional delegation. Unaware that he was observed, Roosevelt slowly lit a cigarette and leaned back, "a smile of complete satisfaction spread over his face." [29]

He was willing to play rough when members of Congress could not be persuaded. Often the dirty jobs were delegated to White House aides, for example, patronage threats and the dangling of postmasterships and dams before fence-sitters on close votes. Big city bosses were sometimes asked to get legislators from their areas in line on

[27] James MacGregor Burns, *Roosevelt: The Lion and the Fox* (New York: Harcourt, Brace and World, 1956), p. 348.
[28] Schlesinger, *The Coming of the New Deal*, p. 554.
[29] Schlesinger, *The Coming of the New Deal*, p. 557.

key votes. He used the veto with the deliberate intent of making Congress respect potential Presidential power, often asking his staff to find something for him to veto. However, he did not browbeat Congress in press conferences and public statements. Cornwell cites the example of the hard fight for public utility holding company legislation in 1935. Roosevelt called for the passage of the bill only once in a press conference and this was at a crucial point in Congressional deliberations when he felt it necessary to act drastically.[30] This was consistent with his policy of not making frontal attacks on Congress.

On balance he preferred to tie his tactical skills to great policy objectives. This was surely the greatest source of his power over Congress in his first term. He picked up the mantle of moral leadership and progressive reform and the nation and Congress responded. Without this aura stimulated by crisis his tactical skill would not have been enough.

Midway in his first term Roosevelt gradually initiated a basic shift in policy that illustrated his political skill and sensitivity. The first New Deal had been based on the gathering of economic interests together under government sponsorship for the collective planning of recovery. The N.R.A., with its codes for business and labor, and the A.A.A., with its planning of agricultural production, were the keystones of this effort. However, he eventually found himself falling between two stools. The Supreme Court declared the N.R.A. unconstitutional and the business community increasingly attacked him as a collectivist. Yet progressive opinion condemned him for setting up planning operations in which large business and large farmers dominated. At the same time Roosevelt came under the intellectual influence of Justice Brandeis, a Jeffersonian atomist, who preached, as he had to Wilson, the virtues of regulated competition in place of national planning. Under these influences F. D. R. concluded that the American people were still in a trust-busting stage of mentality rather than a planning stage, and he gradually shifted his ground, beginning in 1935 and 1936, and the second New Deal began. The shift was toward regulation and away from planning: the Wagner labor relations act, revised banking laws, a reorganized stock market, holding company regulation, the progressive income tax. Roosevelt pushed this legislation through Congress by sheer drive and skill. This shift illustrates how he shaped his legislative strategy out of a larger political strategy. His empiricism and flexibility were seen as

---

[30] Cornwell, *Presidential Leadership,* p. 153.

well. He had not consciously turned left, or right. He did not think in these ideological terms. He was simply responding to new factors and tacking and veering toward unchanged goals. This was Roosevelt, the gay tactician and happy warrior, presiding over a political process that was always close to chaos and loving it.

There was a price to pay for this veering and tacking. Increasingly, Congress became bitter at the President as he manipulated his bills through Congress. Often they were forced to bear the brunt of criticism for his reversals, and more and more they came to feel themselves pawns in his larger game. By the end of his first term he had spent most of his capital with Congress. Before that time political scientist Pendleton Herring had noted the extent to which Roosevelt's control rested on unsteady bases, such as patronage, government funds and favors, the cooperation of Congressional leaders, and the crisis mood of the people. How long, Herring asked, "can the presidential system continue as a game of touch and go between the Chief Executive and congressional blocs played by procedural dodges and with bread and circuses for forfeits?" [31]

The Fox Undone by His Own Craftiness

The classic instance of Roosevelt's undoing by his own cunning was his defeat in his attempt to pack the Supreme Court with pro-New Deal justices in 1937. His overwhelming 1936 election victory when joined to resentment at Court assaults on New Deal legislation caused him to lose his sense of political reality.

His strategic and tactical failures during the Court fight were inherent in his habitual political method.[32] He tried to disguise his attempt to pack the Court by pretending that his plan to appoint an additional judge for every one over seventy who was still sitting was simply a means to greater efficiency in the federal judiciary. He had decided that this approach bore the least political risk. This way of proceeding showed his delight in the secret stratagem, the indirect ploy rather than the frontal attack. But in choosing indirectness he badly miscalculated. The devious method of the reform became more a *cause célèbre* than the substance of his criticism of the Court. He seemed too clever by half.

In the fight with Congress he made one tactical blunder after another. Most of these mistakes can be traced to his overconfidence. He

---

[31] Burns, *The Lion and the Fox*, p. 189.
[32] Joseph Alsop and Turner Catledge, *The 168 Days, the Story Behind the Story of the Supreme Court Fight* (New York: Doubleday and Co., 1938), *passim.*

had not consulted anyone except his Attorney General before he suddenly dropped the plan, like a bombshell. He simply assumed that Congressional leaders would do as he bid. He failed to line up progressive Congressional support in advance or to alert leaders of interest groups who might have supported the plan in the hope of ending Court obstruction of progressive legislation. He had not mentioned the matter in the 1936 election and it came as a shock to the public. His general confidence that the people were with him and that for this reason Congress would defer to him caused him to reject the warnings of Congressional leaders that he would have to compromise. He relied on his personal charm to bring Senate opponents around, a tactic that failed when put to the test. Finally, when defeat was a fact, he found a way out that saved him some face, but his professional reputation with Congress was never the same again.

We cannot say precisely why Roosevelt lost his sense of reality. Overconfidence is a descriptive rather than an explanatory term. Perhaps his inflated ego at times seemed to draw the whole world into its orbit.

Standard Legislative Manipulations That Failed

After 1936 nothing went well in Congress for F. D. R. He seemed to have completely lost his magic. The Court fight was the beginning. The recession that came in the fall of 1937 split Congress into warring economic groups and weakened his electoral coalition. The inability of the administration to find effective remedies for the recession for over a year meant a great loss in political credit. The polls of 1938 showed F. D. R. losing support among low and middle income voters. He kept majority support and his personal popularity remained high, but there was increasing suspicion of his political methods. The old American fear of Presidential "dictatorship" reasserted itself. He had a program for extension of the New Deal but could not get it enacted.

Congress was in open rebellion throughout his second term. Successive legislative defeats were in part reactions against the success of his first term. His very skill was a component of the charge against him. He was said to be dangerous because he threatened the principle of separation of powers. Congress reflected the public fears as well as a concern for its own prerogatives.

There was no diminution in Roosevelt's technical, manipulative skill during his second term, with the exception of the Court fights. But technical skill was of little help when the political tide was moving against him. The New Deal was a spent force. The amorphous, polyglot Democratic party, an electoral coalition, was not reliable for the

President as an agency for the passage of a legislative program. There was little he could do about it except to break away and form a new progressive party. The idea seems to have occurred to him more than once, but everything in the American political system prevents such an attempt, and he wisely desisted.

However, he rode out the storm and prepared the nation for war by use of the same tactical flexibility and resilience that so many of his opponents condemned. And, when war at last came, he was again the lion, the commander in chief who ceased to be a politician and became a world leader.

Administrative Leadership

Roosevelt looked on administrative organization with one question—did it enhance his capacity to rule? [33] His system of command was designed to push the most important decisions to the top. He did this by delegating authority and responsibility in such a fragmented way that the competition below would require decision from above.

Gathering of Information

He did not rely on a single source for information but he used both official and unofficial channels and often set them against each other. He was very accessible for a President. Nearly one hundred government officials could reach him on a direct phone. He read a great number of memos, cables, reports, and even the Congressional Record. His unofficial reading consisted of six daily newspapers and a sampling of White House mail but his chief source of information, both official and unofficial, was from visitors to his office. He used his Cabinet officers and his wife as eyes and ears.

He brought together experts who held a great variety of views and balanced them off against each other. These methods, when added to his fine memory and capacity to store away detail, gave him great knowledge about the operation of government and the state of the country. He was proud of his superior information, perhaps even "stubborn and vain about how much better informed he was than anybody else." [34] This skill "signified the extraordinary receptivity which was one of his primary characteristics." [35]

[33] Richard Neustadt, "Approaches to Staffing the Presidency: Notes on FDR and JFK," *The American Political Science Review,* December, 1963, pp. 855–863.

[34] Gunther, *Roosevelt in Retrospect,* p. 53.

[35] Schlesinger, *The Coming of the New Deal,* p. 526.

Use of White House Staff

He never permitted his personal aides to build up spheres of programmatic influence of their own but gave them functional assignments.[36] They were forced to be generalists and to overlap in their work. Thus, they checked each other and were not threats to him. As generalists he could use them for *ad hoc* purposes, as extensions of himself. In three spheres, no one was given fixed assignment except Roosevelt himself. These were Congressional relations, high appointments, and direct relations with department heads. Whenever he placed reliance on an alter ego, such as Harry Hopkins, it was as an extension of Roosevelt's own power and personality, and one reason Hopkins was so successful as an emissary was that he understood this fact.

Delegation to the Departments

Roosevelt put both Harry Hopkins and Harold Ickes in charge of works relief programs. He ran the Departments of State and War through the undersecretaries and ignored his own Cabinet chiefs. He refused to name single heads of programs, for example, Lend Lease, and the War Production Board for a time, for fear that he would not be able to control basic decisions.

He experimented with various ways to supervise, first trying interdepartmental coordinating committees and discarding this as too unwieldy. Over time, he was the best coordinator of his own administration. He did it well because his talents suited him for it. He had the energy, the liking for varieties of people, the mastery of detail, and the capacity to carry many problems in his mind at once. Roosevelt had little regard for the Cabinet as a unit. Cabinet meetings were seldom worthwhile. Most of his Cabinet appointments were made for political, rather than administrative, reasons. For example, his Secretary of State, Cordell Hull, was valuable to F. D. R. because of his close ties in Congress and the great respect with which he was held by the public. Yet, Hull was often excluded from great decisions of state.

He played Cabinet members and other top officials off against each other. None of them ever felt secure in his service. This insecurity was a function of his view of the Presidency. As he saw it, a President could never put his cards on the table. He had to keep his strate-

---

[36] Neustadt, *American Political Science Review*, December, 1963, p. 856.

gies to himself and leave alternatives of action open. He could never permit a Cabinet officer to committ him to a politically disastrous course of action. He told them that he reserved the right not to rescue them if they got into trouble. He had to protect his Presidential power, even if it meant sacrificing them at times. As he saw it, his position required him to remain above friendship and personal loyalty because the Presidency was not a person, but an institution.

There seems to have been a sense in which Roosevelt enjoyed "the agony below." [37] He could tease his associates unmercifully about their problems. However, he also wanted to make them happy and spent considerable time "handholding," charming, and keeping the peace within his own official family. He liked to refer to himself as "Papa" and enjoyed the role of keeping everyone happy. A sheer love of manipulation is certainly evident here.

Personal Style of Decision-Making

He felt his way toward making decisions, never affirming a policy until his many sensitive antennae had told him the time was ripe, both politically and administratively. This could take months, or even years. He did not decide something was right and then proclaim his support. Rather, he was like a creative artist, who paints a picture without knowing what he will paint. What for others might be an interior debate had to be externalized for Roosevelt, and this could best be done by his process of subjecting himself to all viewpoints.

For him no judgement or decision was final. It was all open-ended. If a policy did not work, it could be adapted. This attitude gave him optimism and confidence. It was rooted in his operational approach to existence.

One drawback was that at times he deceived his associates. He could not bear to say no to them, and, therefore, he often seemed to agree with them when he did not. He often forgot to tell them that he had shifted course after the fact, and he often told conflicting things to different people. In part, all of this was out of a need to protect his Presidential initiative. He could not let himself be pressed or committed too soon. But, if pressed too hard, he would deliberately mislead for the fun of it.

In the long run he was able to keep the loyalty of his associates despite the anxiety he caused them. He encouraged their creativity and gave them free rein. It was known throughout the government that he

[37] Schlesinger, *The Coming of the New Deal,* p. 537.

was receptive to new ideas. He made his catalytic influence felt at every level of government. An agency chief once said, "after spending an hour with the President, I could eat nails for lunch." [38] In the long run, he placed trust in his associates and backed them up and inspired them in the purposes of his administration. He was not a dictator, for he did not issue commands. He never moved until he had a consensus beneath him. So many people had so many fragments of power that they could be brought together for common purposes, not by techniques, but by his moral leadership. In the end, technique was merely the handmaiden of this higher dimension.

Conclusion

F. D. R. and history transformed the Presidency. Radio, and later television, reduced the intimate relationship of Presidents and reporters and made the President the immediate focus of American government for its citizens. Roosevelt pioneered in what could be done with radio to exert Presidential influence in government. Depression, war, and post-war problems ensured that the President would lead Congress in its legislative programs whether he was so inclined or not. White House legislative leadership became institutionalized. The growth of bureaucracy, which F. D. R. began and which followed his tenure, made his kind of freewheeling administrative style unfeasible. The creation of White House executive offices in Roosevelt's second term, with a press secretary, legislative assistants, and administrative aides, was the beginning of the institutionalization of the Presidency. Eventually the Bureau of the Budget, the National Security Council, the Council of Economic Advisers, and other executive agencies came under the White House umbrella.

Roosevelt's strong leadership, in conjunction with events, hastened this institutionalization. This ensured that all future Presidents would have to be leaders. But, it did not ensure that they would be skillful leaders. The President still had the task of asserting personal authority and control. In many ways institutionalization of the Presidency made this more difficult. The President was one step or more removed from the policy-making process he needed to master. By his very search for personal power, Roosevelt, following the path of T. R. and Wilson, had created a new kind of Presidency.

[38] Burns, *The Lion and the Fox,* p. 174.

PART TWO

Introduction

TAFT, HOOVER, and Eisenhower had much in common. They were eminently non-political Presidents.

1. None had a drive for personal power like that seen in the Presidents of Action. Nor did they have self-dramatizing impulses. They shared a desire for order, harmony, and self-restraint.

2. Their needs stimulated them to develop abilities but they were not political abilities. Taft became a good judge, Hoover a fine engineer, and Eisenhower an able military leader. In each case, they emphasized technical skills in their pre-Presidential work and did not spend years developing the skills of moving others by speaking, bargaining, and manipulating as did the Presidents of Action. Hoover and Eisenhower did develop considerable ability to make large organizations work smoothly but this was solely administrative ability in Hoover's case and diplomatic skill in Eisenhower's case. Their philosophies of personal behavior made the manipulation of others by political skill distasteful to them.

3. Each exhibited mental qualities of order, logic, and regularity. They were good with tangible matters but poor at perceiving intangibles. They were strong in structured situations, when they could exercise some control over alternatives, but weak in unstructured situations. They did not enjoy the fast moving political process. They had little tactical skill and lacked the ability to conceive and carry out complex strategies of leadership. Because of their mental traits and character structures they could not ride many horses at once.

4. Their values complemented this style of leadership. Their conservativism often made them skeptical of the need for government action. Their Whig theory of the Presidency undermined their effectiveness in behalf of the ends they did seek. They put great emphasis on personal rectitude and the wrongness of trying to influence others by any means other than reasonable argument. Because they were technical men they overestimated the power of reason in the political process and underestimated the facts of power and conflicts of interest and values. They did not value political craftsmanship.

They were political "outsiders" unlike the Presidents of Action, but they were cultural "insiders" in the sense that they were not marginal men. Each had a stable social identity rooted in the Middle Western boyhood they experienced. They grew up in simple homogeneous environments and were trained in maxims of "Americanism," which they never really lost. This was especially true of Hoover, who lived abroad for some years, and of Eisenhower, who lived within a military world. Cut off from American life in many ways, each held to the simple maxims of his youth. This was the political culture they reflected in their values and character traits. Their view of the Presidency had its roots here.

5. Taft and Hoover did not serve in times favorable to their goals or styles of leadership. Eisenhower was luckier in this regard. Taft ran up against the progressive movement and Hoover against a depression. In both cases, their conservative values and style of leadership were not what was felt to be needed in the White House. This must be taken into account when we judge their skills of leadership. Situations did not favor the exercise of the skills they did possess. Eisenhower benefitted by and helped to create the era of political good feeling in the 1950's. He saw it as one of his greatest accomplishments that he had helped to unify the nation after the harsh political warfare of the last Truman years. This was the kind of skill he valued. In this sense he was a successful President by his own lights.

6. None of these men made important contributions to the powers or operation of the Presidency. Given their Whig theory, we would not expect them to have done so. In different ways, and for varying reasons, each was reluctant to play all Presidential roles to the hilt. Just as they resisted the tide of the progressive movement in its many forms, so did they resist the trend toward greater Presidential power, which was carried along by the Presidents of Action.

CHAPTER 4

William Howard Taft: The Judge

FORTUNE SMILED on Will Taft until the day he entered the White House as President. He had not wanted to be President and would have preferred an appointment to the Supreme Court. However, upon the urging of his wife and brothers, who had political ambitions for him, he acceded to Roosevelt's willingness to secure the Republican nomination for him in 1908. In a sense Roosevelt made Taft President. He also unmade him in 1912.

He was a man with a judicial mind at sea in a political job, and he had been successful in every major public position he held except the Presidency. His other posts had been administrative or judicial. As Chief Justice of the Supreme Court from 1921 to 1930 he was strong and able. But he was not suited by personality for political leadership.

Theodore Roosevelt's innovations in Presidential roles received a setback at Taft's hands. He had no taste for publicity, or for using the press for his political ends. Like T. R. he had to work through the Republican Old Guard leaders in Congress, but he could not and did not desire to handle them as Roosevelt had done. He felt that his predecessor had used his administrative power illegally at times and he was, therefore, careful and cautious in his administrative actions. Roosevelt had made the office one of popular reform, but Taft, more conservative than his old chief, opposed the progressive political trends of the day.

A comparison of Theodore Roosevelt and Taft in the White House illustrates the great importance of personality in the playing of Presidential roles. Not only do we see two men with quite different needs and mental equipment responding to the office in different ways but we also see two political subcultures as they helped shape the conduct of the office. Although of the same political party, Roosevelt and Taft held different conceptions of the Presidency and different norms of leadership.

Taft faced the dilemma that later confronted Hoover. Theodore

Roosevelt caused the public to look upon the Presidency as the lever of popular reform. What does a conservative President do in a time of clamor for reform when he shares neither this conception of the office nor the desire for governmental action? This is one of the unanswered questions for the Whig tradition of the Presidency.

Personality Needs

Theodore Roosevelt had been slightly unpopular at Harvard, because he was different; Taft was the most popular man in his class at Yale.

As a boy and young man he was bright, affable, and full of fun. He was respected because of his honesty and integrity. He did not drive himself and had a tendency to put off work. However, he was not as easy going as he appeared, for he could give way to temper if people took advantage of his good nature.[1]

One of Taft's strongest personality needs was equilibrium. The preference for order over conflict and the inclination to say "yes" rather than "no" were rooted in a certain complacency and affability. Archie Butt, who had stayed on as White House military aide, noted that he had never seen anyone who disliked "discord" as much as Taft.[2] Horace Taft remembered that their mother had often said that "the love of approval was Will's besetting fault."[3] There was a lack of surface toughness and drive in Taft of which he was aware. In a humorous speech to newspapermen, his last speech as President, he said:

My sin is an indisposition to labor as hard as I might, a disposition to procrastinate and a disposition to enjoy the fellowship of other men more than I should.[4]

In 1900 he summed up his attitude toward the judicial bench in a letter to his brother that contained more psychological insight into himself than he perhaps realized:

Perhaps it is the comfort and dignity and power without worry I like.[5]

[1] Henry F. Pringle, *The Life and Times of William Howard Taft* (2 vols.; New York: Farrar & Rinehart Inc., 1939), Chs. 1, 2, 3, *passim*.
[2] Butt, *The Intimate Letters of Archie Butt, Military Aide* (2 vols.; New York: Doubleday and Co., 1930), I, p. 20.
[3] Butt, *Taft and Roosevelt*, II, p. 472.
[4] Pringle, *Taft*, II, p. 853.
[5] Pringle, *Taft*, I, p. 148.

Taft was a judicial man and not a politician. He often longed for the emotional security of the bench in the midst of the insecurity of political life. He was not a self-confident man. Before taking every important post he always doubted in advance his ability to do it. His letters are filled with these self-doubts.

His distaste for political life was a recurrent theme in his letters. While campaigning in the 1906 election as a member of the Roosevelt Cabinet, he wrote his wife: "Politics, when I am in it, makes me sick."[6]

But by 1906, under the prodding of his family, he had become a reluctant candidate for President. Up until the last minute before Theodore Roosevelt secured his nomination he insisted that better candidates might be available. His eighty-year-old mother surely voiced his own sentiments when she wrote him in 1907:

> Roosevelt is a good fighter and enjoys it, but the malice of politics would make you miserable. They do not want you as their leader, but cannot find anyone more available.[7]

Archie Butt summed it all up:

> In many ways he is the best man I have ever known, too honest for the Presidency, possibly, or possibly too good natured or too trusting or too something on which it is hard just now for a contemporary to put his finger . . .[8]

However, beneath the good nature there was rock. Archie Butt recorded that many people around Taft mistook his good nature and complacency for weakness, but they had to learn that "he is as obstinate as a mule and as set in his ways as a Chinese idol."[9] Taft continually vacillated between a complacent yielding to others and a stubborn resolve to go his own way. Henry Stimson, his Secretary of War, concluded that the stubbornness was a defense against the former trait. It was not the stubbornness of a man of firm purpose but of one who sought to protect himself from the purposes of others, for example, the influences of his family.[10] In his Presidential moods Taft alternated between the two polar moods of sunny optimism and a black pessimism. He was most stubborn and least flexible when things were going very poorly. One of his Cabinet officers cited this as "the stub-

[6] Pringle, *Taft,* I, p. 290.
[7] Pringle, *Taft,* I, p. 319.
[8] Butt, *Taft and Roosevelt,* II, p. 515.
[9] Butt, *Taft and Roosevelt,* II, p. 558.
[10] Morison, *Turmoil and Tradition,* p. 180.

bornness of an uncertain man." It was at these moments that the habits, fostered by a judicious mind, seemed to paralyze his will to act. It is not surprising that the good-natured Taft was a strong hater. He was "persistent in his antipathies" and the people he hated the most were those who made things difficult for him, especially maverick` and militant reformers.

Mental Traits

Taft was intelligent, although lacking the agile mind of T. R. or the intellectual power of Wilson. He was solid and thorough and had a passion for exactness. He tended to get bogged down in details and he lacked the ability to make realistic intuitive assessments of situations. His years of experience as a judge and an administrator had perhaps shaped his mental processes in certain ways. He had a dislike of disorder, a desire that business go off as smoothly as possible, and a desire to be in harmony with authority.

These are the qualities of the civil lawyer and the judge. However, not all civil lawyers and judges are this way. These judicious values must have been very congenial to Taft's basic personality, to have been an acculturated overlay on the essential man beneath. Certainly his mental qualities were judicious from the time of his youth. He was slow, thorough, and not given to impulse. His legal opinions reflected this stolidity in their comprehensiveness and lack of brilliance or literary grace.

Values and Ideology

The dominant theme of Taft's value system was the desire for order and stability with legality. Although he was the child of a prosperous, socially prominent Cincinnati family, and was educated much as the two Roosevelts and Wilson were, Taft was not an "outsider" to American life in the sense of being an aristocrat critical of a business civilization. His Middle Western roots were comfortable and he never challenged them. All his life he had a horror of militants and radicals. He was not particularly a friend of the businessman, nor did he enjoy the practice of corporate law. In fact, during the years of his association with Roosevelt, he was a mild progressive. He was certainly never a "reactionary" or an Old Guard Republican.

However, his temperament, mental qualities, and legal and judicial experience spoke for legality, caution, and order rather than for action and change.

He worshipped the law and legal reasoning. He once said that he would rather have been Chief Justice John Marshall than any other American. He abhorred political actions that smacked of extra-legality no matter how desirable the purpose. In this respect he was critical of many of Roosevelt's Presidential acts as being beyond the bounds of legality. Taft felt secure in action only if he thought he had the law with him. He demanded a politics of rectitude. He refused to take campaign contributions from trusts or their officers. He loathed common practices of political patronage. He detested any kind of political "deal." He hated partisan oratory, which distorted the truth, and sought in his own public utterances to always tell the truth regardless of the consequences.

He was basically a "conservative" in his abhorrence of social conflict and his desire for social peace. Although he accepted the progressive thrusts of Roosevelt as President and sought to continue them in his own Presidency, he was not a restless innovator but rather a consolidator who looked on his administration as having the purpose of following up, consolidating, and implementing the Roosevelt reforms. It was not Taft who had changed in 1912, but Roosevelt and the whole reform movement who had moved left. There were two consequences of Taft's conservatism for his political style. He favored quiet, calm methods of leadership and he disapproved of militants and reformers. He abhorred a politics of enthusiasm.

Pre-Presidential Career

In 1900 he surrendered to the request of President McKinley that he head a commission to govern the Philippine Islands. He left the federal bench for this post out of a mixed sense of duty and hope that his reward might be an appointment to the Supreme Court. He was a great success in the Philippines because his position was that of a judicial administrator with very great power. Philippine political culture placed a high value upon the benevolent leader of warm human qualities, and Taft was very popular. He had a strong sense of justice and great skill as a conciliator and peacemaker.

President Roosevelt called him home to be his Secretary of War but he primarily used Taft as a diplomatic troubleshooter, and domestic peacemaker, rather than as an administrator. In the process Taft completely subordinated himself to Roosevelt. Taft took on coloration from his surroundings and associations and, while serving under T. R., he was a progressive. That coloration was to change when he became President.

Political Personality

Taft's needs for ease, agreement, and certainty were complemented by his solid, unimaginative mind, his legalism, and his basic conservatism. He had little positive drive, in either opinion or person. Being essentially passive he put his faith in institutions, the law and the courts, and the Constitution, and took his shape from these anchors. Thus, he was often at sea in unstructured situations and could often be unduly influenced by associates. In his pre-Presidential career he had been an able judge and non-political administrator. In the Cabinet he had done Roosevelt's bidding and had not concerned himself with problems of "power." He had risen to the White House as a result of great personal charm, a good mind, and loyal service and friendship. He was a comfortable man in uncomfortable times. In 1912 William Allen White summed up Taft's conservatism:

It was the natural expression of his character, the reaction upon politics of the temperament of the man who sticks to the facts, sees no visions, reckons only with the powers that be, dislikes pioneering, chooses the soft way out of difficulties, and trusts in material rather than spiritual forces to aid him in extremities.[11]

Conception of Presidency

In March, 1909, Archie Butt wrote in his diary of Taft:

I don't think he realizes yet that for seven years he has been living on the steam of Theodore Roosevelt and that the latter has been his motive power and the things he has accomplished have been largely under the high pressure of Mr. Roosevelt. With Roosevelt out of the country, the President will find, and I think has already found, that his steam has been cut off. He will have to find his fuel now, and, like a child, will have to learn to walk alone.[12]

Taft did realize it. In his farewell letter to T. R. as the hunter left for Africa, he told his former chief, "when I am addressed as 'Mr. President' I turn to see whether you are not at my elbow." [13] As he

---

[11] *American Magazine* (May, 1912), pp. 13–18.
[12] Butt, *Taft and Roosevelt*, I, p. 27.
[13] Pringle, *Taft*, I, p. 400.

went into the Presidency Taft was not at all sure that he was up to the job. It was so different from anything he had ever done. He wrote that were he to be presiding as Chief Justice he would feel at home "but with the troubles of selecting a Cabinet and the difficulties in respect to the revision of the tariff, I feel just a bit like a fish out of water." [14]

He had a somewhat restrained view of Presidential powers. His writings after he left the White House set this view forth in detail, but they corresponded to his actions while in office. He explicitly contrasted himself with Roosevelt in that Taft did not think a President had the right to act in any area unless the law clearly provided that he might. He saw no implied powers to act in the general interest. He favored freeing the President from many "political" tasks. In 1915 he advocated one six-year term, feeling that this would make a President more courageous and less inclined to play politics for a second term. He wanted a permanent civil service and a reduction in the patronage tasks of the President.

He did not want a weak President, but he thought that the President should play an even greater role in Congressional affairs than in the past. He asked that Cabinet officers be members of Congress and applauded Wilson's decision to address Congress personally. These devices, he said, would give the President a greater role in Congressional policymaking. However, he seems to have desired a balance between the President and Congress rather than Presidential domination as Roosevelt desired. Taft wrote in 1915 of the dangers of popular Presidents with large Congressional followings and strong popular support. He said this kind of direct democracy might lead to dictatorship by one man. Here is Taft the classic conservative, fearful of direct democracy, not trusting to checks in the political process itself, and anxious that legal limits protect the rule of law from popular passions. [15]

Leader of Public Opinion

As Secretary of War, Taft had been a favorite of reporters. They would group in his office for friendly background conferences, and he went into the White House with the good will of the Washington press corps but lost it almost immediately. The problem was that Taft was

[14] Pringle, *Taft,* I, p. 378.
[15] William Howard Taft, *Our Chief Magistrate and His Power* (New York: Columbia University Press, 1916), *passim.*

a good lieutenant but a poor captain. He had no ability to shape the news as an instrument of power for himself. He had a very poor sensitivity to currents of public opinion. He was somewhat smug in his judicial posture that he was above news mongering. His abhorrence of drama or emotion prevented his trying to learn the techniques of public relations.

This was true in the 1908 campaign. After the nomination he wrote, "the next four months are going to be a kind of nightmare for me." He was afraid to read the papers for fear that he would have to comment. He wrote:

Those things that can be denied I do not fear. It is those things that have to be partly denied and partly explained that are troublesome.[16]

He was inept in the fight for exposure to public opinion. His mind was too exact and too honest to dissemble. He lacked the gift for the epigrammatic phrase. He detested being in the limelight. In the campaign, he grew discouraged by the criticisms that he was not like Roosevelt.

I am sorry but I cannot be more aggressive than my nature makes me. That is the advantage and disadvantage of having been on the bench. I can't call names and I can't use adjectives when I don't think the case calls for them. . . . I realize what you say of the strength that the President has by reason of those qualities which are the antithesis of the judicial, but so it is with me, and if the people don't like that kind of man, then they have got to take another.[17]

This temperamental antipathy to self-dramatization caused him simply to ignore reporters during his first weeks in the White House. He hoped they were not there. He did not withhold news, as the press began to charge, but simply failed to give out any. He did not have the knack of releasing stories so that the headlines would publicize a Presidential act or opinion, or deflate a Presidential opponent. He felt that to make personality an important factor in the affairs of government was to be demagogic. The judge who believed in rule of law was fearful of any emotional force let loose in politics. He told Archie Butt:

I have made up my mind . . . that I will not play a part for popularity. If the people do not approve of me or my administration after they have had time to know me, then I shall not let it worry me, and I most certainly shall not change my methods. I am going to be honest with

16 Pringle, *Taft,* I, p. 356.
17 Pringle, *Taft,* I, p. 359.

myself, whatever else I do. I cannot be spectacular, and I will not be insincere with those I deal with.[18]

He pursued this basic strategy for four years. Once, when advisers were urging him to stage a dramatic fight over an issue, he bemoaned, "there is no use trying to be William Howard Taft with Roosevelt's ways." [19] Early in his term he had written his old chief:

I have not the facility for educating the public as you had through talks with correspondents, and so I fear that a large part of the public will feel as if I had fallen away from your ideals; but you know me better and will understand that I am still working away on the same old plan.[20]

A result of his refusal to mould the news in his favor was that when it went against him, he put his head in the sand. If the newspapers criticized him, he assumed that they must be wrong. He soon began to develop a persecution complex.

Don't worry over what the newspapers say. I don't; why should anyone else? . . . I told the truth to the newspaper correspondents . . . but when you tell the truth to them they are at sea.[21]

And yet he could confess his own inability to influence the news by writing, "I suppose the public has difficulty in getting what it is all about." [22] The fact that he was following the colorful Roosevelt was of course a problem. People often, unjustly, called Taft to emulate T. R.'s methods, unmindful of the fact that Taft was a different man. But this fact only made the problem more acute.

He lacked a sense of the President as a political strategist who must create bases of support for himself, and use that support as a lever for Presidential power. Taft did not like to be unpopular, and he could not abide criticism, but he did not have the strong need for popular favor that drove Roosevelt to become a master of public relations. He was quite objective about it. Toward the end of his term he wrote:

It is a very humdrum, uninteresting administration, and it does not attract the attention or enthusiasm of anybody.[23]

Taft felt no natural affinity with audiences nor was there any ham in him. One of the first things Archie Butt noticed after the new

[18] Butt, *Taft and Roosevelt*, I, p. 298.
[19] Butt, *Taft and Roosevelt*, I, p. 235.
[20] Pringle, *Taft*, I, p. 401.
[21] Pringle, *Taft*, I, p. 53.
[22] Pringle, *Taft*, I, p. 474.
[23] Pringle, *Taft*, II, p. 603.

President was inaugurated was that he seldom took any notice of crowds gathered to see him as he was traveling. Butt concluded that Taft would never "care a hang about this form of popularity." [24] His formal tours were somewhat more successful for Taft in terms of striking up a rapport with audiences, simply because a President on tour is likely to be an object of affection and Taft was not the kind of man that anyone could actively dislike. But he lacked Roosevelt's natural exhibitionism, and dreaded having to write and make speeches.

He committed some classic blunders of public relations, the most memorable of which was the Winona, Minnesota, speech in which he carelessly defended an inadequate revision of the tariff and by so doing widened the split in the Republican party and weakened his own position.

In September, 1909, he began a Western tour that had as its purpose the healing of the split in the party between Old Guard East and the Progressive West over the new tariff law. The insurgent picture of Taft by this time was of a reactionary President who had joined with the Old Guard leaders. Taft would not prepare his speeches sufficiently in advance, but he waited until the last minute, as he had all his life with work that did not absorb him. The major result was the disastrous Winona speech in which, without taking thought, in a hastily prepared speech, he described the tariff as "the best bill that the Republican party ever passed." The body of the speech was a reasoned defense of the bill, but that one phrase, taken out of context, made the headlines and ruined the entire trip. Yet, he had thought it his best speech because it set forth his position truthfully. After the Winona speech the progressives were completely alienated from Taft.

A second error on that tour was Taft's behavior toward Speaker Cannon for whom he had little use. Taft took a steamboat ride down the Mississippi with the Speaker and treated him like a long lost friend. Archie Butt saw it and wept:

> The President simply hates him and expressed his contempt for him wherever he can do so, yet he openly flattered him on the trip down the Mississippi, was photographed with his arms about his neck, and appeared to endorse him wherever they spoke together.

Taft was trying to get Cannon defeated for the Speakership, Butt observed:

[24] Butt, *Taft and Roosevelt,* I, p. 18.

. . . yet he constantly gave him strength by appearing to approve both him and his actions.[25]

Taft was always adding to his difficulties by political ineptitude. When Gifford Pinchot, the government's chief forester, became convinced that Secretary of the Interior Ballinger had acted contrary to the public interest in Alaskan public land decisions and, along with other progressives, began to attack Ballinger, his superior, and by implication Taft, the President did nothing except to caution Pinchot. Taft was anxious not to offend Roosevelt by harming Pinchot, T. R.'s conservation colleague. The effect in the long run was that Pinchot was openly insubordinate, and Taft had to fire him. But at no time did Taft directly attack Pinchot and those criticizing Ballinger, even though he believed Ballinger to be right. He simply avoided any open conflict, hoping that the public would somehow learn the truth themselves. Taft was content to suffer in silence. He told Butt:

> Of course Roosevelt would have come back at those preferring the charges and would by now have them on the run, but I cannot do things that way. I will let them go on, and by and by the people will see who is right and who is wrong.[26]

Later when Louis Brandeis and a Congressional committee began to publicize evidence relating to Guggenheim influence in the Alaskan lands, Taft took no public action. Archie Butt remembered that he just sat silently and grew morose.[27]

In a speech after the 1912 election a mellow Taft, who was happy to be leaving the White House, frankly analyzed his weakness as a figure in the spotlight.

> One of the results of my observation in the presidency is that the position is not a place to be enjoyed by a sensitive man. . . . The result in some respects is unfortunate in that after one or two efforts to meet the unfounded accusations, despair in the matter leads to indifference and perhaps to an indifference towards both just and unjust criticism. This condition helps the comfort of the patient, but I doubt that it makes him a better patient.[28]

In short, Taft treated his publicity problems in the White House as a private man would, seeking to protect himself from accusations, resentful at attacks, despairing of answering back, and having no sense

[25] Butt, *Taft and Roosevelt,* I, p. 20.
[26] Butt, *Taft and Roosevelt,* I, p. 235.
[27] Butt, *Taft and Roosevelt,* II, p. 694.
[28] Pringle, *Taft,* II, p. 844.

of his official stake in dominating the news for the uses of Presidential power.

Legislative Leader

Taft once wrote: "I am not so constituted that I can run with the hare and hunt with the hounds." [29] He came into office pledged to achieve the Roosevelt policies of 1906 and 1907 and by the end of his term he had made a modest success of this goal. But the reform movement had not stood still, and eventually neither did Roosevelt. Taft discovered that, once out from under the influence of T. R.'s force and magnetism, he was really a conservative and he began to draw the line on reform and to side consciously with Republican conservatives. This was political disaster. Taft was out of sympathy with rising tides of opinion.

In addition to his conservatism and his political ineptness and laziness, all of his judicial qualities were a handicap to him as chief legislator. The "ordinary legal mind" operates from fixed principles, seeks to be consistent with past precepts, and sees men and issues in polar aspects of right and wrong. These qualities lead to a strong inflexibility. Taft was typical of this mentality. He liked to adopt a hard and fast stand and castigate opponents as acting in a way contrary to law. Given this mentality and that of the progressive Republicans, conflict was inevitable.[30]

Taft's legislative style could be summed up in three phrases: achieve results, avoid drama, and keep integrity. He did not think in terms of building political capital for himself and then using that capital as a lever of influence. He went into the power struggle without weapons except that of his own good will and his persuasive powers. He seemed to think that the political process was an arena of reason rather than of power. From the beginning he resolved to act as if he only had one term:

I believe too, that it is good politics. If I stand for anything, it is for being straightforward and natural, and it is unnatural to try any other role.[31]

By taking this course he ruled out from the beginning many standard techniques of influence. He was loathe to use patronage to in-

---

[29] Pringle, *Taft,* II, p. 411.

[30] George E. Mowry, *The Era of Theodore Roosevelt* (New York: Harper and Row, 1958), p. 266.

[31] Butt, *Taft and Roosevelt,* I, p. 260.

fluence members of Congress. He appealed to the public over the heads of Congress only as a last resort. He sought to placate and bind to himself the Old Guard leaders in Congress and put his trust in them as the best means to get his program through. His creed was— don't play politics, fight for what is right, and seek to be a source of unity rather than of discord and eventually other leaders and the public will follow along. Taft sought to be a model of integrity rather than a mover of power.

Taft put his basic strategy in a letter to *Kansas City Star* editor W. R. Nelson in 1909. Roosevelt had been a crusader, he said, but now the task was to put that reform into legal execution. Lawyers were best fitted to do this and he had therefore put many lawyers in his Cabinet. He was confident, he said, that the Congressional leaders would cooperate in a way that they might not with a radical Cabinet or program. He was pursuing this cautious policy because he was anxious to achieve something instead of just making pronouncements and ending up with nothing to show at the end of his term. He said that he much preferred to be criticized as a reactionary than to give way to the progressive appeal for militant reform now and have nothing to show for it. They were a minority and he could not rely solely on them.[32]

This was a strategy dictated in part by Taft's situation. Roosevelt had made the same initial decision to cooperate with the leadership and move slowly in his demands. However, Taft's strategy of leadership was also based on his predispositions. He abhorred drama and disliked conflict. He disliked militants of any kind. He relied on the good faith of others and was anxious for stability. These predispositions were to shape his strategy in a way quite different from Roosevelt's. Whereas T. R. had been able to play various groups off against each other, Taft was seldom able to assume the initiative. He spent much of his time in defensive fighting after his expectations about the cooperativeness of Congressional leaders were upset.

Taft seemed incapable of acting out of a considered strategy. Boldness, which in another President might have been strength, in Taft was too often rash imprudence. And it was usually followed by timidity. He began his Presidency with a rash act that Roosevelt would never have committed. Angered by Speaker of the House Cannon's speeches mocking downward tariff revision, to which Taft was publicly pledged, the President sought to unseat Cannon. Roose-

[32] Pringle, *Taft*, I, p. 382.

velt advised him not to do so because failure would mean trouble, but Taft acted from personal pique rather than political strategy and he gave House progressives the notion that he was with them in their efforts to unseat Cannon and reduce the Speaker's powers. Taft had not started the campaign and he was not consistent in his support of it. At a crucial moment in the fight Cannon, Aldrich, and others of the Old Guard called on Taft and told him that he could not have tariff revision if Cannon were defeated. However, in return for support for Cannon, the party organization would follow his lead on the tariff. There was little Taft could do but agree; the insurgents were so outnumbered. The progressives concluded that Taft had deserted them. Cannon was reelected Speaker with Tammany votes. However, during the tariff debate that followed Taft felt that Cannon had not lived up to his pledge and he again let it be known that he favored his unseating.

House insurgents were again mystified and angered by Taft's wavering. This resentment was compounded by the fact that Taft and the Republican organization simultaneously deprived the progressives of good committee assignments and patronage and revealed that insurgents would be officially opposed in the 1910 primaries. When challenged about this Taft answered that the reformers were harming his programs and the Republican party and he could only conclude they were opposed to him. He had reason for anger at the progressives, for they had attempted to revise his programs, but it was contradictory to oppose simultaneously both Cannon and Cannon's enemies. Eventually, when the House did curb Cannon's powers, Taft got no credit, but only the mistrust of progressives.[33] As he had said, he could not run with the hare and hunt with the hounds.

The passage of the Payne-Aldrich tariff illustrates Taft's ineptness. He felt strongly about the need for downward tariff revision and had made it central to his campaign. However, he failed to make a strong plea for such action in his 1909 message to Congress. He told friends privately that he was already on record on the matter, so why bother to restate it? The tariff reductions passed in the House but in the Senate Aldrich began to raise the rates on important items to benefit Eastern industry. Progressive Middle Western Senators launched a massive attack on the Aldrich bill. Taft's dilemma was whether to side with the Senate minority, with whom he agreed, or to support Aldrich and the great majority of Republican senators? For a short

[33] Mowry, *Era,* pp. 239–241.

time he tried to work both sides. He met with the rebels and gave the impression that he was with them. He thought about appealing to the public and talked of vetoing a high tariff bill. He might have used patronage as a club but refused to do so. Neither did he appeal to the people. He did not know how to play, or enjoy playing, a complex game of legislative manipulations. Taft was hindered by his lack of political sensitivity and his tactical clumsiness, by his conservatism, which made him reluctant to attack American industry, and by constitutional scruples about interfering too much in the legislative process. What was worse he told Aldrich that he had such scruples. In the end he decided that Aldrich was sincerely trying to lower the tariff.[34] As had always been the case before, he put himself under the influence of the strongest personality in his environment. He found the insurgents too distasteful to link himself with them and, out of his growing liason with Aldrich, decided to put his trust in the regular Republican organization. At the time he said privately to aides that he was dealing with "acute and expert" politicians who might deceive him. He struck a bargain with Aldrich that he would discourage an income tax bill in return for which Aldrich promised the reduction of the highest rates in the conference Committee. However, Taft weakened his hand by telling reporters that he would not denounce the high rates publicly and would not veto a bad bill. Such actions would only give him a lot of "cheap publicity," he said, would hurt the party "and the only person who would gain popularity would be your humble servant." [35] Taft did succeed in getting reductions after hard fighting, but the final product was a high tariff designed to benefit Eastern industrialists at the expense of producers of raw materials in the South and West. Nothing could have been better designed to split the Republican party. However, Taft thought it a good measure, as his disastrous Western tour revealed. His lack of political sensitivity was such that he did not really appreciate the spontaneous popular opposition to the Payne-Aldrich tariff throughout the country. This episode, like the Cannon case, illustrates his ineptness, conservatism, and legalism. All were handicaps to Presidential influence in Congress.

The principal strategic failure of Taft's Presidency was his inability to hold his party together or make it an effective legislative instrument. The situation and his conservatism were more to blame for this than his political and legislative ineptness. However, his clumsiness was

[34] Mowry, *Era*, p. 245.
[35] Pringle, *Taft*, I, p. 437.

such that it seems doubtful that he could have been an effective leader of Congress under any circumstances. A few examples will suffice.

On one occasion Secretary of War Henry Stimson was fighting a Congressional attempt to write legislation setting forth criteria for the Army chief of staff that would eliminate Chief of Staff Leonard Wood. Stimson prevented one attempt by getting Taft to write a letter to the congressmen involved. When they tried it again, Stimson told the President and instead of getting angry Taft said, in a rather sad way, "I don't see why they should try to do that to me again." [36] Taft was willing to accept Congressional assurances that they meant no harm to Wood but Stimson forced an admission from them that they, in fact, did mean harm. Stimson was anxious for Taft to publicly threaten a veto, but he would not and only implied it "politely" and ineffectually. Finally Stimson goaded Taft to tell a key senator he would veto the bill as it stood, and the matter was dropped. Stimson's conclusion on the incident was that Taft had caused himself and others "enormous unnecessary trouble" because "he would not strike out from the shoulder." He felt that the President had "very little heart in his task." He said that at moments like these he had to act with Taft, "as if I were taking his fist and trying to drive it forward for him." [37]

Archie Butt, a shrewd judge of character, summed it up:

> So much in the President's character can be explained by his complacency. He believes that many things left to themselves will bring about the same result as if he took a hand himself in their settlement. He acts with promptness and vigor when he has got to act, but he would rather delay trouble than seek it.[38]

However, at times, out of obtuseness, Taft could seek trouble. Roosevelt had never tried to raise second class postal rates even though the government was subsidizing the periodical press. T. R. had needed the "muckrakers" and their journals. But Taft entered the fight for upward revision, and incurred the hostility of much of the periodical press.

Another of his crusades came in 1911 with the fight for reciprocal trade with Canada. At times he could be stubborn when he felt strongly about an issue. He ignored Elihu Root's advice to forget the issue and secured passage of a bill by making a deal with the incoming Democratic House majority. The agricultural products of the South

[36] Morison, *Turmoil and Tradition,* p. 166.
[37] Morison, *Turmoil and Tradition,* p. 167.
[38] Butt, *Taft and Roosevelt,* I, p. 202.

were not threatened by Canadian exports but Middle Western farmers and Eastern protectionists were strongly opposed. Taft thus succeeded in alienating all groups in his party and further splitting it.[39] Eventual Canadian rejection of the treaty was perhaps prompted in part by the President's impolitic phrase in a speech that Canada and Great Britain were coming to "the parting of the ways."

Taft's administration was not without legislative achievement. From 1910 to 1913 there was considerable piecemeal reform. Much of it can be credited to a coalition of Democrats and Republican progressives. However, even here Taft showed his ineptness. He went into two fights with essentially the same position as Congressional progressives and succeeded in alienating them both times. He favored the Mann-Elkins bill for railroad regulation but when progressives attempted to improve his bill, he concluded that they were opposed to him. Both he and progressives favored federal postal savings banks but when they again sought to modify his notions, he resented it. He reduced his political capital in both cases.[40] Most of his energies during his last two years in office were taken up in worrying over the progressive-conservative split in the Republican party and the threat to his own position occasioned by the return of Colonel Roosevelt from the wilds of Africa. It was not a comfortable time for any President but Taft was singularly ill-fitted for riding the wild horses within the Republican party. His dislike of conflict, basic conservatism, tendency to respond to the strongest forces in his environment, dislike of militants, and growing resentment of Roosevelt all caused him to cling to the right wing of his party and to seek to do little except ride out the storm. One cannot say what a more vigorous President might have done in such a situation. Theodore Roosevelt, in the last months of his rule, had foreseen the party cleavage and then, and later, taken up the mantle of progressive leader. This was a role Taft could not play by personality or conviction.

Administrative Leader

Francis E. Leupp summed up Taft as an administrator in 1910 in a comparison of him with Roosevelt:

Their fundamental theories of administration are fundamentally diverse. Mr. Taft's is the more dignified, Mr. Roosevelt's more human. Mr. Taft's conception of the government is of a gigantic machine, its many parts so

[39] Mowry, *Era*, pp. 284–289.
[40] Mowry, *Era*, pp. 259–261.

articulated as to be moved from a single source of energy; and the engineer confines his attention to this central distributing point. As Mr. Roosevelt sees it the government is an organization of live men, each engaged in doing something which, if not well done, diminishes the efficiency of the rest; hence when he was in command of this legion he had his eye on the corporals not less than on the captains. Technically speaking Mr. Taft follows the more orderly method when he communicates only with his cabinet officers and leaves to them the direction of their subordinates. . . .[41]

The judicial mind preferred a structured chain of command and a passive stance of dealing only with the top echelons. But the same pattern of passivity and complacency seen in the rest of his political style emerges here. Archie Butt remembered that Taft was a loose administrator in the War Department and he left most of the details to subordinates and thereby let the department develop many warring factions.[42] It must be remembered that Taft was not an administrator as such as Secretary of War but was used by Roosevelt on outside missions. However, Taft does not seem to have been a vigorous administrator. He complained that Roosevelt had shown little respect for official channels and had often dipped into the lower echelons to deal directly with lesser officials. By inference, Taft himself preferred the normal chain of command and delegation of authority to top subordinates. In 1911 his brother, Charles Taft, complained that the President let his Cabinet run riot with him. There was no coordination among them. They wanted to run their own departments and be left alone, and several of them simply defied the President. This was all a result of Taft's original intention to hold his Cabinet members solely responsible for departmental policy, his brother felt, with the result that each had grown arrogant in his place and none had helped Taft politically. He recommended that Taft fire one member, thus bringing the others into line. But the President always refused to fire Cabinet members for political reasons.

Stimson remembered that Taft was often too willing to listen to advice before reaching a decision and therefore Cabinet officers found it relatively easy to exert influence on him.

Certainly, Taft preferred technicians to politicians in his Cabinet, as seen in the high number of lawyers among his original Cabinet. But he had trouble controlling his Cabinet officers politically. He kept up a running battle with Postmaster General Hitchcock over Southern

[41] *The Atlantic* (November, 1910), pp. 648–53.
[42] Butt, *Taft and Roosevelt,* I, p. 386.

appointments and usually lost to him, so that in 1912 Taft was dependent on Hitchcock for control of Southern delegates in the Republican convention. When Ballinger finally left the Cabinet, Taft appointed a new Secretary of the Interior without learning that he was a LaFollette supporter. Again we see the old predisposition to trust and the old disinclination to probe.

Part of the reason for Taft's restrained style of administrative leadership was that he felt Roosevelt had often acted illegally and he was determined not to do so. Taft was always careful to have explicit legal justification for all of his administrative actions. Just as he was distrustful of the emotional insurgents in Congress so did he find the holdover Roosevelt crusaders distasteful. He thought Pinchot was a wild fanatic and his distaste for Dr. Harvey Wiley of the Pure Food and Drug administration, was just as great. However, Taft characteristically did little to curb these "troublemakers" and Archie Butt remembered that he was very reluctant to discharge Roosevelt people and put his own people in. Political expediency probably was a factor in this, but his great complacency was perhaps another factor. Butt felt that Taft had little desire to make a whole series of new appointments. He preferred to take the line of least resistance, and of course it caused him trouble in the long run, when the progressives in his administration burst the bonds.

In general his administrative style reflected his "political personality" in its calm, judicious, and somewhat passive stance. He wanted non-political administration with as little conflict as possible.

Perhaps his most serious weakness, not only as an administrator, but also as President, was his laziness. He ate too much, wanted to sleep too long, preferred bridge to work, and was always reluctant to leave the golf course. He would spend long hours in idle conversation with political visitors without any strategic end in view. He loved travel because it got him out of Washington and away from problems but complained that he was expected to make speeches on his tours. He complained to Archie Butt that there was so much to do and so little time in which to do it, but it was his own fault. He did not really like doing many of the things a President must do and was not willing to work hard at the job.

In 1911 Taft permitted the government to file a suit against United States Steel in which it was charged that the steel magnates had deceived Roosevelt in the 1907 panic when they had asked permission to purchase a company in order to quiet the panic. Taft did not know of this specification until it was too late, but its effect on Roosevelt was to hit his sensitive ego, drive him into a rage, and precipitate his candidacy. Perhaps it was a matter beyond Taft's normal control, but he should have been aware of the political sensitivity of such a suit and have examined the briefs himself. He never asked to see them. He had no ability to see the interrelationships of politics and administration. And besides, he was lazy.

Conclusion: Chief Justice

Taft's essential strength fully manifested itself in his work as Chief Justice. This serves to 'emphasize the basic point that a good judge is not necessarily a good President.

On becoming Chief Justice he did not experience the self-doubts that had plagued him on the assumption of every other position. As Chief Justice he worked harder and longer than in any job he had ever held. One sign of his buoyancy was that he kept his weight under control. Always before in his life, his weight had gone up in periods of unhappiness and no more so than in the White House years.

As President he had failed in many attempts to persuade the politicians and the public to support his ideas, but, as Chief Justice, he was very effective in persuading Congress to enact measures of judicial reform.

He dominated his colleagues on the court and worked very hard for a unified court. He did not like dissenting opinions, and often he held his own views in restraint and refused to write a dissenting opinion himself when he might have split the court by so doing. He judged potential justices not so much in terms of their philosophies as by their cooperativeness. His old dislike of troublemakers was still evident. Here was the essential Taft, the orderly, judicial arbiter, who disliked discord, and loved the life of the bench in which conflict and self-expression were rigidly hedged in by an ancient system of law and custom. He was a much stronger Chief Justice than President because his skills were judicial and not political.

CHAPTER 5

Herbert Hoover: The Engineer

HOOVER'S NOMINATION for the Presidency by the Republican Party was an example of the occasional popular demand for a man above politics in the White House. Republican Party politicians did not want him as the nominee in 1928 for they feared he would not be sympathetic to their viewpoints. But much of the public, especially most Republicans, seemed to want him so far as we can tell. This was because of his favorable image as the "great engineer" and the "great humanitarian." He had proved himself to be a master at running large-scale organizations before and during the war. In the 1920's, as Secretary of Commerce, he had become almost a folk hero, the embodiment of the national values of prosperity and efficiency. This was not love of Hoover the individual, for he was stiff and formal in public and averse to personal publicity. But the image the press gave of Hoover as the supreme technician made him popular.

Eisenhower was to benefit from an image created by the press during and after World War II. The contents of the two images were different but the results were the same. Each man was nominated for the Presidency without actively seeking the office, on the strength of his image and on the basis of achievements outside political life. In both cases, their conception of the office was a non-political one.

Hoover wanted to be President in order to complete the programs for the rationalization of American economic life that he had begun as Secretary of Commerce. He thought of the Presidency as an administrative task. In 1928 a few skeptics warned that he was not qualified for political leadership but this did not seem important or even relevant in a time when Presidential leadership seemed to be administrative rather than political.

The depression ruined Hoover's political image precisely because he could not pick up the challenge of political leadership that it set. He could not inspire, dramatize, or engage in effective legislative fighting. He tried to handle the crisis as if it were solely a problem of administrative planning. As a result, much of the public turned against him. Eventually, Franklin Roosevelt filled the vacuum in popular affections.

Hoover sought to be a strong, active President within very rigidly defined bounds. He wanted his will to prevail over Congress but he set limits to the means he would use to make it prevail. He ran a tight administrative ship but he had little sensitivity to the political implications of administration. He had no political sense, no eye for intangibles, and no ability to manipulate. He wanted to run the Presidency as one might have run a giant corporation in the 1920's, as a world unto itself.

His ideology handicapped his Presidential skill. His depression programs went further than any President had ever gone in enlarging the role of government in economic life. But, he had difficulty admitting this. He was fighting history and F. D. R. finished the job and took the political credit.

Hoover's lack of skill cannot be blamed on the depression. Any President would have had great difficulty leading in the first years of that crisis. But he showed a lack of political skill even before the depression. We can only conclude that he was a strong man and excellent administrator who was unqualified for the top political job.

Political Personality

Herbert Hoover was born in the Quaker community of West Branch, Iowa. Orphaned at an early age, he lived with relatives in Iowa and Oregon until he entered Stanford University to study engineering. The orphan, the frontier Quaker, and the engineer: these are the three keys to the young Hoover.

The death of both parents before he was ten must have been a harsh experience for the boy. This could help explain the quality of constraint in his personality, his tendency to hold things in, to resist displays of emotion in himself or others.

He grew up in a Quaker community and absorbed its values. His dislike of show and exhibitionism, his intense hatred of combativeness and discord, his desire to be of practical service to others, with emphasis on the practical, his basic trust in human goodness, and his insistence on the importance of cooperation in the human community were all undoubtedly derived from his Quaker roots.

However, the fact that he was a Quaker will not by itself explain his character traits. His basic values of service and rectitude were of Quaker origin, but his rigid self-control and his strong drive to give shape and form to external objects were of a special personal intensity.

As a mining engineer he was exceptionally talented. His mind had always run to quantitative subjects, mathematics and science, and he was poor at verbal studies, failing English all four years at Stanford. Throughout his life he doodled on scratch pads, and the doodles were linear designs without words. He enjoyed encompassing the real world in designs and boxes of his own making. As a student at Stanford he revealed his organizational talent. He became a student leader, not because of magnetism or popularity but because of his great organizational skills and his selflessness in service to student groups. He was the manager of the football team and the treasurer of the student government. In those jobs three qualities, which were to appear in later years, reveal themselves. He had a strong drive to organize other people. He had the capacity to inspire loyalty in others. He had a tendency to take all the burdens of a task onto his own shoulders.

His career as an international mining engineer was brief but fabulous. He rose to the very top of his profession. He combined his great organizational skills with his drive to experiment and innovate. He was a revolutionary in his development of new techniques. He displayed his old ability to win the loyal support of his co-workers, including the miners in the pits. He developed a lifelong tendency of idealizing his vocation of the moment in terms of universal values. He slowly formed an ideology of capitalism that was to be his firm anchor in years ahead. Its essence was a celebration of man's productive genius. It was a creed suited to his temper. Of his mining years he wrote:

Ours was a happy shop. There was the sheer joy of creating productive enterprises, of giving jobs to men and women, of fighting against the whims of nature and of correcting the perversities and incompetence of men.[1]

The "great engineer" could easily become the "great humanitarian" who organized and ran the Belgian food relief organization in World War I. Thereafter, he was United States Food Administrator in the war and director of food relief to a starving Europe in the post-war period. He became a world figure, one of the few men to emerge from the war with lasting prestige. In 1914 Hoover had been giving thought to retiring from engineering and devoting himself to public service. His Quaker strain dictated it. The Belgian disaster gave him the op-

[1] Herbert Hoover, *The Memoirs of Herbert Hoover, Years of Adventure, 1874–1920* (3 vols.; New York: Macmillan Company, 1952), I, p. 100.

portunity. The successive wartime jobs were made to order for the Hoover talents. He created massive organizations of spirited volunteers and ran them with a smooth but iron hand. He created great loyalty in numbers of men who were to flock to his banner in later years. He got the job done with a genius for picking the right subordinates, for coordinating countless myriad activities, and for driving hard against obstacles, material or human, until they gave way. In each successive post he laid down one prior condition, that is, he be given the power to direct the organization as he wished. He was something of a benevolent autocrat who preferred to hold all the reins in his own hands, to master all the data himself, and to mould the organization in his spirit. He had great confidence in his own constructive intelligence, in the scientific collection of knowledge as a guide to action, and in the willingness of men to respond to facts and appeals to their good will.

It was during the war years that he thought through his ideology of "American individualism" and as Secretary of Commerce in the Harding and Coolidge administrations he implemented it. The ideology itself was essentially a statement of the American economic, social, and political system as he understood it. Hoover based it on the principle of free individualism. The economic system blossomed because of individual initiative. The social system was not based on class but on individual mobility and opportunity. The purpose of government was not to dominate, but to regulate so that individual liberty might be enhanced. He was never a devotee of *laissez-faire*. But he always feared the power of the central government as a potential threat to individual liberty. Therefore, he advocated voluntary restraint and regulation and local and state action whenever possible. He felt that free energies must not be stifled.

Aside from the content of this ideology, two points are important. Hoover looked on this creed as a "system," like a logical engineering construct. It could not be accepted or rejected except as a whole, and therefore he held it with a certain rigidity. In addition, he transferred his urge to "form" the world from engineering to social life. He was more a "former" than a "reformer." Just as he enjoyed the touch of a giant organization, so did he yearn to shape American society in line with his model of the ideal potential of the unique American system. This was the drive that sent him into government. The Department of Commerce had been a minor, fact-collecting agency, but Hoover turned it into the strongest office in the Cabinet and made himself the major figure, next to the President, in both administrations.

Hoover insisted to President-elect Harding that, as Secretary of Commerce, he be given a voice in all matters of economic policy. The result can be seen in Hoover's memoirs. In a long series of chapters he relates his activities as Secretary of Commerce in the fields of foreign affairs, finance, labor, and agriculture.

Hoover's goal at Commerce was to encourage the rationalization of American economic life in terms of greater efficiency, productivity, cooperation, technological development, and elimination of discord, all to the end of realizing his goal of a continuously expanding economy that would eliminate poverty. He convened commissions of experts, called together representatives of many industries and businesses, and encouraged self-regulation and improvement in industrial technology. He called for some legislation to promote these goals but emphasized voluntary compliance rather than government coercion.

In the process of this amazing career he further enhanced his reputation in the eyes of the American public as a miracle worker and organizational genius. This was a natural extension of his wartime image. Both seem to have been the product of journalistic enterprise. Hoover shunned personal publicity, but as Secretary of Commerce he did give wide publicity to his many achievements through the use of press releases. However, he consistently steered clear of politics and it was as a non-political man that he ran for the Presidency and won. Hoover, like Taft, might well have thought twice before he became the chief politician of the nation. He must have known that political leadership was not his strong point, but he wanted to be President because he wanted to finish the job of giving shape to the "American system" as he conceived it. He was still the engineer.

Personality Needs

He was orderly, scrupulous about details, and kept a tight rein on displays of emotion. His strongest drive seemed to be to organize and give shape to human activities, to impose rationality, as he conceived it, not only on organizations but also on persons. Perhaps this drive was a function of the inner need for order, but we cannot know. In any event, the drive was very intense.

Mental Traits

His mind was that of the engineer, in love with logic, system, and mental constructs, lacking in intuitive touch, with a tendency to press

facts into molds. He had a mind like a card index and a great capacity
to absorb facts. The systematic quality of his mind and his need for
order complemented each other, and they surely influenced each
other in the process of development.

Values and Ideology

His ideology had two broad components, those of rectitude and
conservatism. Characteristically he thought of himself as not in "politics" but in "public service." It was all very selfless, the Quaker obligation to serve one's fellows. He was a hyper-moralist and rationalist
in politics, automatically distrusting political deals and manipulations,
and fearful of the appeals to mass emotion in political life. One of the
persistent themes of his memoirs is his complaint that his appeals
to reason were constantly being inundated by the demagogy of the
opposition.

He held to a spiritual materialism, a common American culture
trait. Although he never said that the goal of American life was a
chicken in every pot and a car in every garage, as he was supposed
to have said, he could have said it. In a message to the Republican
national convention in 1964 he pointed to deprivations of the civil
rights of Negro Americans but added that they undoubtedly owned
more cars than the entire Soviet population. Always a utilitarian,
Hoover was insensitive to the intangible forces that drive men, and this
was a great handicap to him as a political leader in time of crisis. His
personality was a unity. His mental qualities reinforced his psychological drive for order and vice versa and his high idealism and
ideological fervor were of a similar cast. These forces clung together
because of his strong drive to force a unified pattern of order and
consistency, not only within himself, but also on the world. Was this
a defense against inner chaos? We cannot say, but to bring order out
of chaos was what he saw as his life's work.

Conception of the Presidency

Hoover believed in a strong President but one bound by definite
limits. He came into office with a great number of well-prepared programs, which were, for the most part, extensions of his work at Commerce. In his eyes, the role of the President was to be a strong leader
in presenting such programs for public and Congressional approval.
But he pulled back from any conception of the President as a strong

manipulative leader or dramatist. In his memoirs he criticized the view that the President is supposed to go beyond advising Congress and is expected "to blast reforms out of it . . ." [2]

> I felt deeply that the independence of the legislative arm must be respected and strengthened. I had little taste for forcing congressional action or engaging in battles of criticism.[3]

In recounting his struggles with the Democratic Congress from 1930 to 1933 he expounded:

> No matter how much emotion a President may feel at all these aberrations of the democratic process, he cannot or, at least, should not display it lest he injure the process itself. There was a choice of two courses: The one was to battle publicly with the Democratic-controlled Congress; or to do one's best to cooperate, consult, explain, and implore, with the hope of getting somewhere.
>
> I have felt deeply that no President should undermine the independence of legislative and judicial branches by seeking to discredit them. The constitutional division of powers is the bastion of our liberties and was not designed as a battleground to display the prowess of the President.[4]

However, within these limits, Hoover thought of the President as a strong executive who dominated the governmental process. He wanted and expected to dominate Congress, regardless of what he wrote about the matter, but he hoped to do it without fighting, simply by structuring information and argument and his expert authority in such a way that Congress would comply with his wishes. His posture was strong and positive. But he was distrustful of process and inept at political manipulation and therefore his practice was often weak.

Leadership of Public Opinion

Hoover, like Taft, was a favorite of reporters when he was in the Cabinet. They went to his office often to talk freely and off the record. He provided a good grapevine, as one who would chase down stories for them about other departments. He impressed them with his encyclopedic knowledge of government affairs. Gradually, an impression came through from the press to the public that Hoover was the best informed man in Washington. These meetings with newsmen were successful because the top job was not his. Reporters did not put pressure upon him and he did not have to weigh every word for

---

[2] Hoover, *Memoirs,* II, p. 216.
[3] Hoover, *Memoirs,* II, p. 217.
[4] Hoover, *Memoirs,* III, p. 104.

political effect. He was at his best when he could casually unfold his extraordinary knowledge. He was engaged in little political controversy in his work and could use newsmen to advertise his many reform schemes.

However, just as Taft had discovered, Hoover found that the pressure of the Presidency required skills of manipulation of the press and public opinion for which he was not prepared and which were not congenial to him. He began badly in the 1928 campaign because he felt that reporters' questions were too prying and openly showed his resentment. After the inauguration White House promises for improving contact with reporters were not developed and, increasingly, throughout his term Hoover substituted the press release for the press conference.

The mechanics of White House press relations were poorly handled. Hoover delegated this to a series of incompetent press secretaries who often attempted to impose censorship on reporters. He himself developed an increasing pique about the attempts of reporters to cover every phase of his activities. He failed to use the press as an instrument to inform the people or to increase his own political capital. He often withheld facts or actually misstated facts. These tactics, of course, angered reporters and only increased the vicious circle of antagonism.

In the Department of Commerce he had been so accustomed to having his public statements accepted without question that the transition to the hot seat was uncomfortable. More than this, he was willing to use the press as a propaganda mill for himself, but he was neither able nor willing to conceive stories and slogans for reporters in such a way as to increase his own political influence. His old dislike of flux revealed itself. He wanted to secure a consensus on policy solutions before he released news, and he was afraid to let the genie out of the bottle. In speeches and in private letters he made it clear that he disapproved of the tendency of the press to look for fights within the government because this only made everyone's job harder, and he feared the effects on the public of press misinformation before the entire truth could be assembled and given out by the administration. In short, he wanted to structure decision-making and inform the public in terms of his habitual style of influence, the dominance of leaders and publics by his superior knowledge. The press, on the other hand, finds the free-for-all political process more congenial. Naturally newsmen want information that decision-makers seek to deny them, but, instead of playing the game, Hoover retreated into his fortress and pulled up the moat. Another reason for his attitude was his sensitivity to criticism. He read the papers carefully and had them clipped. Critical stories and columns pained him. There were instances of his trying to have reporters discharged. He played favorites with the White House correspondents. These basic antagonisms were intensified by the depression, not only because of the wear and tear on Hoover, but also because his public stock went steadily down and caused him to regard the press with even greater suspicion. The explanation given in retrospect by Hoover and his associates for his poor press relations is that he felt it necessary to work in secret on depression recovery plans for fear that premature disclosure of weak spots in the economy would start the very public panic he sought to avert.

There were certainly instances when this was a realistic approach. If a number of banks were in a precarious financial position, the President could not advertise the fact in requesting Congressional action to shore up these institutions. In his memoirs Hoover gives many instances of this kind of situation with plausibility. His policy of calling conferences and preparing legislative proposals in great secrecy had a wider justification, that is, he wanted the people to believe that the depression was in large part a frame of mind. If public optimism could only be restored, confidence would return and the nation would pull itself out of the slump. Therefore, Hoover deliberately put himself in the strange position of a public herald declaiming that prosperity was just around the corner when he actually had great private forebodings about the situation. For this reason he did not think it right to play up the darker aspects of the depression in his pleas for legislation or his discussion of achievements.

These justifications for a policy of quiet are only partly convincing. In the first place, Hoover's perennial optimism fooled no one and made him look ridiculous in the eyes of the public. Also, his refusal to publicize his activities gave the public the impression that he was doing nothing to fight the depression, whereas, in fact, he was working day and night, seven days a week. And finally, he tied his own hands in his efforts to influence Congress by his refusal to dramatize. Hoover, of course, did not see it this way, but there were many opportunities for giving the nation a dramatic picture of recovery through the Hoover policies that he failed to take. It seems likely that Hoover's policy of quiet was a rationalization of his distaste for drama and the limelight and his fear of discord.

When his aides urged him to dramatize a particular matter his reply invariably was, "This is not a showman's job. I will not step out of character." [5] Often he would say, "I can't be a Theodore Roosevelt" or "I have no Wilsonian qualities." [6] He was always intensely uncomfortable when he was personally in the spotlight. He wrote of himself on his return as a hero to America in 1919:

I have never liked the clamor of crowds. I intensely dislike superficial social contacts. I made no pretensions to oratory and was terrorized at the opening of every speech. [7]

He overcame his fear of speaking, but retained his dislike of crowds and hoopla. His admiring biographers and former aides frankly attribute this to shyness. His press secretary wrote that "He was not quite his true self in public." [8] He was stiff and ill at ease and always read from a prepared manuscript. It would follow that the same was true for the dramatization of ideas and programs. By contrast, he knew that he was most effective in persuading others in small groups with his comand of facts and his quiet, charm, and sense of humor, which rarely if ever showed in the public Hoover. Hoover, the great engineer, the humanitarian, and even the progressive Secretary of Commerce, had a certain glamour enhanced by the myth-making skills of American journalism. But Hoover the President was gray and drab. All of Hoover's former associates are agreed that his shrinking from personal publicity was due to his temperament and that it was a political handicap for him. Had the depression not occurred he might have once again have been "sold" to the public as an efficiency expert in the White House, a myth designed to appeal to the national intelligence but not to its heart. But he was not up to the difficult task of self-dramatization in the midst of chaos. Arthur Krock bemoaned his "awkwardness of manner and speech and lack of mass magnetism," as a result of which there was no passionate loyalty for him in either party or public. [9]

He insisted on writing his own speeches, agonizing over each phrase and word, aiming at exactness rather than color or emotional· effect. His press secretary said that "the principal criticism to make of his

[5] Theodore G. Joslin, *Hoover Off the Record* (New York: Doubleday and Co., 1934), p. 2.

[6] Schlesinger, *The Crisis of the Old Order*, p. 243.

[7] Eugene Lyons, *The Herbert Hoover Story* (Washington, D.C.: Human Events, 1959), p. 23.

[8] Joslin, *Hoover Off the Record*, p. 7.

[9] Harris G. Warren, *Herbert Hoover and the Great Depression* (New York: Oxford University Press, 1959), p. 130.

addresses is that each one was too correct in detail, too precise, for the casual listener or reader." [10] He preferred facts to adjectives, laced his remarks with statistics, and deliberately refrained from appeals to emotion. His style of delivery was, to say the least, unmoving.

He rarely used his press conferences to make appeals to the public for support on given issues. In his State Papers only fifteen of the seventy-six statements included could be classified as appeals to Congress for action or condemnation of action already taken. His radio addresses are included in the State Papers and very few dealt with the general explanation of policy. Most were ceremonial. In his talks to the nation Hoover ". . . either could not or would not get beyond the level of highly generalized exhortation, or the enunciation of vague aspirations and moral precepts." [11]

Hoover's limitations as a leader of public opinion were a function of all the strands of his political personality: his mental traits, his self-effacement, and his distrust of appeal to emotions. He thought the public should be interested in a man's principles and in a documented case rather than in broad pastels. His speeches were full of information and were intended for a public seeking intellectual enlightenment. But they gave little to a nation in distress seeking assurance for its fears and a torch for its hopes. The great engineer could not inspire.

Legislative Leader

Most of the men who worked with Hoover agree that he lacked political skill. One told Eugene Lyons that he seemed "out of character" in the political arena. Another said that "the ways of the politician were never quite clear, and, on the whole, distasteful to the chief." [12] Hoover's lack of political skill was the obverse of his good qualities. He was a man of reason and rectitude who addressed himself to problems in a rational way and appealed to others in those terms and not in terms of the actual perspectives held by congressmen and others in the political process. He felt a certain disdain for the Congressional leaders, even of his own party, and they sensed this and returned his feeling in kind. But more important than this, he had no gift or inclination to appeal to others in any terms other than those of high patriotism and pure reason. He could not forge support for himself out of the imperfections of other men.

[10] Joslin, *Hoover Off the Record,* p. 44.
[11] Cornwell, *Presidential Leadership,* p. 113.
[12] Lyons, *Hoover,* p. 27.

He was very firm and insistent in pressing his views on Congressional leaders and quite stubborn in rejecting their alternatives. In no sense was he a weak leader. The central flaw in his legislative leadership was that he was not willing, and probably not able, to employ a strategy of manipulative leadership in Congress. This was contrary to his values, and uncongenial to his personality. He simply pressed his plans on Congressional leaders in a somewhat stubborn fashion, again and again, until they were either accepted or rejected, usually *in toto*. Theodore Joslin, his press secretary, remembered that Hoover prepared all depression recovery plans by himself, and always to the last detail. Then, if Congressional support were required, he would summon Congressional leaders to the White House and outline his program to them. If it were acceptable to them he would produce a statement for publication that he had already written. He did not discuss with them what kind of an announcement should be made. Hoover never presented a program unless he was certain that it was valid. He deliberately refrained from offering programs for political effect. After he had invested much time and energy in the preparation of his programs it was not easy for him to be flexible in regard to Congressional revisions. As Joslin put it, with unconscious irony, ". . . he always had a plan, for any and all contingencies, tucked away in his brain or his coat pocket. But most of the time he experienced difficulty in inducing others to agree with him." [13]

He bombarded his conferees with his great knowledge, often using the material gathered by the many commissions he appointed. Joslin says that Hoover believed that Congress was primarily a number of committees and commissions set up to investigate and determine legislative policies. But Hoover also wanted special bodies to be used as barriers against half-baked legislation. He wanted the widest possible use of experts. During his administration he appointed sixty-two commissions. Evidently, he did not acknowledge the existence of a political process in which compromise and bargaining had a legitimate place. He was quick to condemn the political process as playing "politics" contrary to the national interest. His image of the Congressional politician was that of a selfish demagogue. He had great respect for Congress as an institution and almost no respect at all for its personnel. This led to his paradoxical stance toward Congress. He exalted it as an institution but in practice sought to exclude it from the policy-making process as much as possible. He wanted acquiescence in his

[13] Joslin, *Hoover Off the Record*, p. 107.

plans. This suggests that his reluctance to take stronger measures against Congress, for example, to stage dramatic fights or try horse-trading, or various Presidential levers like patronage, was due to his repugnance for the political process as much as it was due to a concern for the integrity of the legislative branch. He was simply behaving as he had behaved in all his previous positions. He supervised the gathering of facts, and, once they were gathered and analyzed, he could not believe that all those exposed to them would not make the same deductions from them as he.

Joslin remembered that Hoover always sought to avoid controversies and fights. He once told Joslin, "a man should not become embroiled with his inferior." [14]

Hoover's legislative difficulties are often attributed to the depression. Certainly any President in his position would have had the same problems he had with the Democratic Congress of his last two years. However, just as he revealed his ineptness at public relations before the depression struck, so did he damage his professional reputation as a legislative leader in his first months in office.

In the spring of 1929 the new President called Congress into special session to redeem campaign pledges of relief for agriculture and tariff revisions to help the unprotected. Eventually he secured the creation of the Farm Relief Board to cushion the uncertain market for farmers. To do so he had to abandon a stated tenet that a President should never interfere in the legislative process. When the Senate ignored his advice on a key provision he issued a critical public statement, summoned Congressional leaders to the White House, and demanded action on his terms. He succeeded because he was riding on the capital of his victory and public prestige. Hoover knew how to get his way by ordering. Would Congress always defer?

In the fight over the tariff it did not. He was politically naive to think that mild upward revision in behalf of agricultural producers and depressed industries would be possible. Instead, Pandora's box was opened and the President lost control. His own Congressional party split into warring bands and he did not seem to know how to respond. Although his ideas on revision were very close to those of Senate insurgents who fought the logrolling of Old Guard Republicans, he would not intervene or speak out. His public reputation began to suffer as a result. Only once did he issue a public statement, to defend Presidential power to change rates from the threat of Con-

[14] Joslin, *Hoover Off the Record,* p. 20.

gressional emasculation. Then, he lapsed into silence. *Time* magazine reported that his "apparent uncertainty" on tariff rates had become a standing joke, in spite of his careful explanation that it was not his duty to legislate on such matters.[15] Democratic attacks on his fumbling impressed the country that he was weak and indecisive.

Finally, by the firm, private exhortation of Republican leaders he was able to secure passage of a bill, but it reduced the President's power to change rates and increased duties on many items. Messages poured in from economists, business leaders, and so forth, urging that he veto it, but he reluctantly signed it. He put on the best face he could by maintaining that the President and tariff commission were henceforth empowered to make scientific adjustments in rates. This was wishful thinking. Final passage did not come until June, 1930, after the depression had hit, but Hoover's loss of reputation in the matter was unrelated to the depression.

He wanted to prevail over others in the administrative ways that were congenial to him. This was the conclusion reached by Walter Lippmann:

> My own notion is that a close examination of Mr. Hoover's conduct in critical matters will disclose a strange weakness which renders him indecisive at the point where the battle can be won or lost . . . this weakness appears at the point where in order to win he would have to intervene in the hurly-burly of conflicting wills which are the living tissue of popular government; that he is baffled and worried and his action paralyzed by his own inexperience in the very special business of democracy.[16]

He tended to panic if he thought Congress was going to fight him, or make life difficult for him. In February, 1930, he became alarmed at the many expenditure bills that had been introduced in Congress. This was, and is, an old practice in which spending bills are thrown into the hopper to please constituents even though their authors know that they stand no chance of passage. Hoover, understanding little of the group life of Congress, took this seriously and had aides count up the proposed expenditures and then publicly produced the figure of a necessary forty percent increase in taxes to meet these measures. Members of Congress were amazed and chagrined that the President would attack a straw man. He then tried to quiet the storm by absolving Congress and holding the public and interest groups respon-

[15] *Time* (March 3, 1930), p. 13.
[16] Walter Lippmann, "The Peculiar Weakness of Mr. Hoover," *Harpers* (June, 1930), p. 3.

sible. This did him little political good. He took the edge off his own attack by shortly thereafter requesting one hundred million dollars for the Federal Farm Board, and again in May he asked Congress for twenty-eight million dollars for new public buildings. The House responded to this leadership by voting, in an election year, veterans and rivers and harbors benefits, over Hoover's objections. But he had not handled his own requests properly. In December, 1930, after Democratic victory in the Congressional elections, he again used panic language to warn of possible Congressional "raids on the public treasury." *Time* magazine reported that some observers saw Hoover as turning over a new and bolder leaf and adopting Rooseveltian tactics against Congress, while others saw him as a nervous, sensitive man who had been swamped by his own anger at the loss of support.[17] The evidence supports the latter conclusion. Hoover was on edge from the failure of recovery, the election defeat, and Congressional unruliness. Congressional Republicans did not rise to defend his blast but, rather, sent the Senate majority leader to complain that they had not been told in advance and that their advice must be sought if Hoover wanted their cooperation.

Hoover's greatest mistake in his attacks on Congress was to accuse it of irresponsibility at a time of national crisis. He lost friends in both parties as a result. His action seems to have been dictated by a deep distrust of legislative men and processes.

As *Time* put it in their evaluation of the President at midterm: ". . . he has come to think of himself as a martyr, in a hair shirt, misunderstood and misinterpreted by the people." [18] As they saw it, Hoover was a victim of the Superman image that had been created in the 1920's. The country had been warned by criticis of his political ineptitude but in the summer of prosperity no one cared for political skill. Hoover was the Great Engineer. However, the tariff and other fights made his ineptness clear. He moved quickly to respond to the stockmarket crash, summoning economic leaders and pressing voluntary agreements to keep jobs, and wages up and prices down. He spoke in terms of restoring confidence and predicted the crisis would be short-lived. When it continued, his prestige dropped, but he continued to make optimistic statements. In short: "His irrational effort to divorce government from politics explains many of his difficulties and is, as was predicted in 1928, his most serious defect as President.

[17] *Time* (December 22, 1930), p. 8.
[18] *Time* (March 2, 1931), p. 12.

For, although he calls government an art, he doggedly continues to act as if it were a science." [19]

In October, 1931, Walter Lippmann noted that Hoover was still indecisive and hesitant about dealing with political issues and "extraordinarily fertile, impulsive and energetic in trying to influence matters that lie outside the duties of his realms and power." [20] Thus, in meeting the depression, Hoover had been most at sea in using the political potentialities of the Presidency. He was disinclined to act strategically and bewildered by political opposition and public criticism. However, he showed the greatest confidence and boldness in attempting to guide the nation's industrial life. This was seen in the conferences of economic leaders that he called and the voluntary guidelines he laid down for their action. He was happiest when he could be Secretary of Commerce or Food Administrator again. These were areas actually outside the normal range of Presidential duties.

After 1930 Hoover fought many standoff battles with the Democratic Congress. He did not hesitate to veto or to stand fast. His initial strategy had been to try to commit Democratic leaders to his "non-partisan" recovery programs in advance. The future Speaker of the House, John Nance Garner, said frankly that party politics and policy differences prevented such a liaison. This dashed Hoover's hope of non-partisan government presided over by himself.

Arthur Schlesinger points out how Hoover actually abandoned many of his convictions in responding to the depression, but denied that he had done so. He leaped from one fixed idea to another, some of which were contradictory, and held to each with great rigidity. He was wont to damn all counterproposals as not only dangerous to the American way of life but also as insincerely conceived and as directed to harm himself politically. He denounced reciprocal trade agreements as "a violation of American principles." [21] He charged with petulance that Senator George Norris and other advocates of public power were "socialists" and were simply trying to create such havoc in the utilities field that socialism would be the only way out.[22] Even though he did not like federal action in many emergency areas he permitted himself to extend federal responsibility further than any President ever had. Yet, he continued to denounce those who wanted to go a bit further. Schlesinger asks:

[19] *Time* (March 2, 1931), p. 13.
[20] *Time* (October 12, 1931), p. 11.
[21] Schlesinger, *The Crisis of the Old Order,* pp. 230–247.
[22] Hoover, *Memoirs,* II, pp. 302–303.

How could he be so certain where was the exact line of demarcation between beneficent intervention and limitless evil? . . .

In the end, Hoover, dragged despairingly along by events, decided that wherever he finally dug in constituted the limits of the permissible. Doctrinaire by temperament, he tended to make every difference in degree a difference in kind and to transform questions of tactics into questions of principle.

As his term wore on, the ideological obsession grew. He had himself done unprecedented things to show the potentialities of national action; but anyone who went a step beyond transgressed the invisible line and menaced the American way of life.

His was the tragedy of a man of high ideals whose intelligence froze into inflexibility and whose dedication was smitten by self-righteousness.[23]

Hoover could not see facts that were not provided for in his conceptual framework. For example, years later he wrote that during the depression "many persons left their jobs for the more profitable one of selling apples."[24] There is convincing evidence that Hoover simply shut his eyes to the fact that private local and state unemployment relief efforts could not do the job.[25] It did not fit his theory of self-reliance at the community level as the basic American creed. He frequently quoted statistics on the success of local relief programs that were belied by any personal observation at all. He trusted too much to his own habitual methods of gathering information, for example, government statistics and the reports of those with a vested interest in relief operations as they then existed. Nowhere was Hoover's rigidity more apparent than in his resistance to federal relief action, and this probably more than any other factor lost the 1932 election.[26] Carl Degler, who has made a study of this matter, concludes that Hoover "was temperamentally incapable of doing what a politician has to do, i.e., admit he could be wrong and compromise."[27]

The sense of popular hatred of him wounded Hoover and perhaps helped confirm his intellectual rigidities. He did not like to talk with people whose views were different from his own, but only with people whom he knew in advance would agree with him. In his memoirs he could see no mistakes committed during his Presidency. He saw himself as fighting not just to save the country from the

---

[23] Schlesinger, *The Crisis of the Old Order,* p. 246.

[24] Schlesinger, *The Crisis of the Old Order,* p. 241.

[25] Warren, *Herbert Hoover and the Great Depression,* pp. 196, 197.

[26] Warren, *Herbert Hoover and the Great Depression,* p. 208.

[27] Carl Degler, "The Ordeal of Herbert Hoover," *Yale Review* (June, 1963), p. 580.

depression but also for the survival of American institutions against those who would wreck them with demagoguery. As a lame duck President he pushed Congress hard to enact his anti-depression recommendations even though he had just been repudiated by the public.

His pre-election conferences with President-elect Roosevelt were seen by Hoover as opportunities to publicly commit Roosevelt to Hoover policies. When Roosevelt refused to do this, Hoover became convinced that he was not only ignorant but also a dangerous man. This ideological rigidity was obviously a handicap to him as a legislative leader. It was a function of Hoover's temperament, his logical, comprehensive mind, his political creed, and the fact that he was President at a time in history when the tenets of that creed were crumbling under attack and crisis.

Administrative Leader

Many observers noted that as President he had great ability to keep many projects moving at once, keeping in close touch with each, and coordinating them all in terms of a unified pattern in his own mind. He was an activist for rationalization and order, who looked on government as "the greatest business on earth." [28] His use of expert commissions reflected this drive. He wanted to apply scientific method to social thought "as correctives to indiscriminating emotional approach." [29]

Many of his administrative acts when he first became President revealed his sureness of organizational touch. He made many good administrative and judicial appointments. He increased the White House secretariat and thus added to his efficiency. In this sphere, in which he was largely autonomous, the initial hesitation of his relations with Congress was absent.

In the summer of 1930 a serious drought killed cattle and crops throughout the Southwest. Arthur Schlesinger comments that "this was Hoover's sort of problem—Belgium all over again, so much more concrete than the irritating and intangible issues of depression." [30] The journalist Mark Sullivan who was Hoover's intimate wrote that the President turned to fighting the drought ". . . with something like a sense of relief, almost of pleasure." [31] The steps that

[28] Hoover, *Memoirs,* II, p. 218.
[29] Lyons, *Hoover,* p. 246.
[30] Schlesinger, *The Crisis of the Old Order,* p. 170.
[31] Schlesinger, *The Crisis of the Old Order,* p. 170.

he took to combat the drought show his talent at galvanizing others into cooperative action. He persuaded the railroads to give half-rates on feedstuffs, directed expansion of federal highway construction to aid unemployment, called a White House meeting of concerned governors that had requested a Congressional appropriation for feed loans to farmers, persuaded banks and insurance companies to extend mortgages, and raised money for the Red Cross for needy families. In his memoirs he recounts these exploits, beginning each sentence with the words "I did. . . ." This was a revealing clue to the man. There was a subtle authoritarianism in his administrative style. He tended to assume that he had to take the entire burden for important action upon himself, and associates and subordinates were simply instruments in his hands. This brings us to certain "compulsive" traits in his administrative style. Hoover personally read and approved every letter sent by the Bureau of the Budget to executive agencies "clearing" their individual replies to Congressional inquiries on legislation.[32] In this one act several of Hoover's traits can be seen: the reluctance to delegate authority, the tendency to immerse himself in detail, the tendency to assume that only he could ensure wise governmental action, and a certain distrust of his own associates.

He did not enjoy critical advice from anyone and showed only mild enthusiasm for the single Cabinet member who differed vigorously with him, Secretary of State Henry L. Stimson. There is no evidence that any of his Cabinet advisers altered his direction or his pace or presented him with counterproposals in meeting the depression. Fenno concludes: "Hoover's temperamental sensitivity, his intellectual superiority and his personal reserve all would tend to reduce critical advice." [33] Hoover literally initiated all of the policies of his administration. Cabinet members simply implemented them. Joslin remembered that Hoover "had almost no one to aid him. By that I mean men of wide vision who could conceive broad plans and make them operative. He had to do it all himself." [34] Dominance of all decisions down to details best suited his personality. There was a certain arrogance in Hoover, wearily but willingly taking the weight of the world on his shoulders. Stimson's biographer describes Hoover's entry into the 1932 campaign: ". . . as always, he set about this immense task as if he alone must do it without the help of others." [35]

[32] Neustadt, *Presidential Power,* p. 210, n. 4.
[33] Fenno, *The President's Cabinet,* p. 278.
[34] Joslin, *Hoover Off the Record,* p. 144.
[35] Morison, *Turmoil and Tradition,* p. 416.

There was certainly a compulsive quality in his drive for control over all aspects of a task.

Hoover almost never, if ever, acted impulsively. He wanted to know where he was going before he made a decision. So the process of decision-making was a long, slow discarding of alternatives until a solution finally emerged. This sometimes took days or weeks or months, and during this time Hoover would work twelve- and eighteen-hour days, seven days a week, wearing out experts and giving unceasing attention to all details himself. For example, in the limitation of fleets among the United States, Britain, and Japan, Hoover personally mastered the minute details of fleet tonnage and the intricate equations of arms limitation by number. Stimson remembered that during these periods Hoover was beset by moods of indecision, which were terribly wearing on everyone around him. But, once he had developed a solution, he was extremely reluctant to see it altered. This was perhaps a function of his inner need for order. Once order had been achieved by the adoption of a plan, he was not prepared to reintroduce chaos by modifying the plan. Hoover also had a certain egoism of ownership in his ideas. Stimson remembered that since Hoover conceived the idea of a moratorium of war debts by himself he was very reluctant to have the British share in putting it forward before an international conference.[36]

It is only conjecture but perhaps much of the aspect of "living hell" during Hoover's Presidency was not so much due to the depression as to his isolation and loneliness in the eye of the hurricane. Franklin Roosevelt was a joyous President during the same depression. But Hoover had to solve all the problems by himself. He insisted on working in secret. He could not inspire either a party following or popular support. To read the record of his incredible labors in the White House, meeting after meeting, conference after conference, working well past midnight, and so forth, is to get the impression that Hoover thought that he could solve national problems by sheer personal exertion.

Conclusion

Hoover's political personality was a unity—needs, mental qualities, and values complemented each other. This political personality made him a great administrator and organizer but he never should have

---

[36] Morison, *Turmoil and Tradition*, p. 361.

succumbed to the ambition to become President. He did not have the kind of normal political drives that a President should have. However, the urge to refashion America in line with his vision was too great. Had he not given in to this urge, his public career in administration might have been greatly prolonged and his public reputation maintained.

CHAPTER 6

Dwight D. Eisenhower: The General

EISENHOWER, like Taft and Hoover, brought with him to the White House ideas about leadership that had been formed in a professional career. He had been supremely successful with these conceptions and said often during his Presidency that he intended to adhere to tried and true methods of persuasion and administration. We can see his style of leadership as Supreme Allied Commander in World War II reproduced, in its essentials, in Eisenhower as President.

In accordance with his ideas he built up the institutionalized Presidency by entrusting the White House staff, and especially his Chief of Staff, Sherman Adams, with great authority. He created a Cabinet secretariat to record Cabinet meetings and to help implement Cabinet decisions. He gave considerable emphasis to the National Security Council as a decision-making body. All of this was rooted in a conception of collegial leadership, which, some critics have felt was harmful to the personal authority of the President. The charge has been made that Eisenhower created buffers and barriers between himself and the policy-making process and thus reduced his potentialities for personal power. His successors have reduced this institutionalization in part, but they have also kept some of it and utilized it differently. This suggests that Eisenhower's distinctiveness was not so much in his liking for the institutionalized Presidency as in his disinterest in a search for personal power in the Presidential chair.

By his own lights he was a successful President who came to the office to give it administrative coherence, to create a climate of political unity in the country, and to convert the Republican Party to policies of moderation. He succeeded, for a time, in achieving all of these things. There was an interesting paradox to this, however. A majority of the public gave him credit for these achievements but a majority of those who are politically active in Washington, even some within his own party, gave him low marks for political craftsmanship. Of course, he did not value such craftsmanship if it were to be interpreted in terms of the skills of manipulating other men and accruing Presidential power.

He did not create a set of precedents for political craftsmanship for succeeding Presidents in the Whig tradition. He failed to grasp the role of party leader and therefore did little to make over the Republican party in his own moderate image. This would have been a difficult task at best, but he did not try. He went into the White House with extremely deferential ideas about his proper relationship to Congress. He had to learn through experience that Congress would not be cooperative without a certain amount of Presidential assertiveness, but he learned the lesson too late to set a good example of skill of leadership for his tradition.

In addition, his style of administrative leadership, while it did succeed in freeing the President from many petty details and burdens, was retrogressive in the sense that it did not, in the minds of many critics, solve the enduring problems of Presidential control.

Eisenhower was a nearly perfect embodiment of the Whig tradition in its strengths and weaknesses. He was a strong person, with well-formed ideas about how to lead, who sought to be a non-political President. Partisanship, conflict, bargaining, and popular emotion were all distasteful to him. The result was that, in the playing of Presidential roles, he did not develop a sensitivity for power and he therefore lacked a certain political skill. His virtues were great—his honesty, reasonableness, desire to build bridges to all groups, and his obvious sincerity. But these were personal traits and they vanished with him. He made no enduring contribution to the Presidential office or to the Whig tradition. That tradition needs to have impressed upon it a respect for political craftsmanship. Eisenhower failed to provide the model. One can hope that a politically experienced Republican leader will one day, as President, provide those guidelines.

Political Personality

Those who have gone to Abilene, Kansas, in search of information about the young Eisenhower have discovered the incipient traits of the mature man. He had a logical, orderly, empirical mind. His brothers remembered that Dwight's mind was like that of their father because it was completely logical, as logical as mathematics. He had a passion for facts, and liked to know the exact name for things. Vagueness annoyed him and he seemed to have a drive to eliminate ambiguity in favor of certainty.

His most outstanding personal characteristic seems to have been his great personal charm. Everyone liked Ike because Ike liked everyone. He radiated sunniness and optimism.

There is general agreement that the youth showed no desire whatever to dominate anyone. Raised with five brothers in a cooperative family atmosphere, he seems to have developed very early a trait that was to be strong in his style of leadership, that of the team player who saw his contribution as only that of one among several. He was adaptable to the wishes and needs of others. He seemed even then to have the special quality of empathy that later was his hallmark. However, he had great self-confidence and inner integrity that at times produced stubbornness. He would not permit others to walk over him. He seems to have hated conceit in himself or anyone else and to have disliked flattery directed toward himself.[1]

When General Eisenhower returned to Abilene in 1952 to run for President, he described the virtues of his parents, integrity, courage, self-confidence, and unshakable belief in the Bible, and asked, if each of them would dwell on these, would not world problems be made simpler?

Would we not, after having done our best with them, be content to leave the rest with the almighty, and not to charge all our fellow men with the fault of bringing us where we were and are? [2]

Milton Eisenhower said years later that his parents held to this simple faith in moral redemption as the basis of social order and that he could never convince them of its inadequacy.[3] They were members of the Church of the River Brethren, a Mennonite group. In the River Brethren Church scripture was interpreted not by a clergyman but by groups of the faithful through discussion. The conscience of the individual was the final test of judgment. The emphasis was on external plainness and inner piety. Dwight Eisenhower was never to lose this belief that things could best be set right if men of good will would only come together to do right. His thought and actions would always lack an appreciation of the darkness in men, and of the need to sometimes raise sanctions against them. Power as a fact of life was not a part of this vision.

Army Career

His ability to command men was seen during World War I, when after graduation from West Point he commanded a tank training

---

[1] Kenneth S. Davis, *Soldier of Democracy* (New York: Doubleday and Co., 1945), pp. 66, 67, 85.

[2] Bela Kornitzer, *The Great American Heritage: The Story of the Five Eisenhower Brothers* (New York: Farrar, Straus and Cudahy, 1955), p. 27.

[3] Kornitzer, *American Heritage*, p. 277.

battalion. He showed the two traits that were to mark him: great organizational skills and the ability to create a high morale among an entire unit.[4]

After that he had little direct command of troops, much to his regret. He became a staff officer, an organization man. He stood first in his class at the Fort Levenworth Command and General Staff School, and was thus tabbed as an expert on logistics and planning.

Eisenhower was a child of the army staff system. Under that system the commander exercised a broad control over the organization beneath him, which in turn supplied him with the information necessary for his decisions. The commander would make decisions on the basis of alternatives presented by his staff officers, and the staff would implement them. The man at the top sought to be free of details and to conserve his energies for the big decisions. There was no problem of power. Orders were sufficient. Delegation of authority downward was a doctrine taught in army schools. Subordinate commanders were to be given assignments and latitude in finding ways to carry them out. The ability to delegate was the mark of a good commander, and it followed that he must take the blame for the failures of his subordinates and give them the credit for their successes.

Supreme Allied Commander

Eisenhower commanded the greatest army in world history but most experts are in agreement that his unique role and his claim to greatness were due to his organizational and diplomatic skills, rather than to any strategic talents. He created the atmosphere of Anglo-American military unity out of which strategic decisions could be made. He encouraged the solution of disputes not by orders, but by reasonable discussion at all levels of the chain of command. It was his firm conviction that such an organization, which combined two nations, could function, not by enforced authority from the top, but from strong feelings of loyalty to the team and its mission. He had the ability to draw subordinates to him by his quality of selflessness. Talented field generals like Montgomery, Alexander, Patton, and Bradley or airmen like Tedder and Spatz knew that Ike was no threat to them, knowing rather that he sought to give them maximum latitude, praising them when they succeeded and taking the blame when they failed.

Eisenhower was also skilled as a referee between the different

[4] Davis, *Soldier of Democracy,* p. 166.

military arms. It is generally agreed by military writers that he did not set basic military strategy so much as he held the entire organizational effort together, especially in planning and logistics, the fields in which he was a master. But, in strategy he seems to have primarily acted as a coordinator between the Combined Chiefs of Staffs of the two nations, and Roosevelt and Churchill, and his very capable field commanders.[5]

There was a sharp edge to Eisenhower's style of leadership, and it was found in his Chief of Staff, Walter Bedell Smith. Smith was a tough, crusty officer who complemented Eisenhower's warmth and good will and thus supplied the element of sanction to Eisenhower's decisions that was perhaps lacking in the persuasive method. Smith's personality and the job he did for Eisenhower bore a striking resemblance to the role later played by Sherman Adams as Chief of Staff to Eisenhower in the White House. The two men were much alike, and their tasks seem to have been the same: to shield the General from undue pressures and demands that others sought to make upon him, to say no in ways that the General would or could not, to follow up the decisions of the General in implementation, and to be an extension of the General in many areas of decision.[6]

Eisenhower always dominated his staff, but he used it to free himself from details, to free himself for time to think about important questions. Over and over again he would comment to aides on how he needed more time to think, on how so and so was taking a great load off his shoulders by assuming charge of a certain area of work, and so forth. His mind worked in such a way that he needed time to reflect, to balance factors, and to fit a specific decision into the total, ongoing strategy. All of this reflected his desire to lead in an orderly, logical, coherent way.

There was a reverse side to this strategy of leadership. The very personal qualities that made him a success as Supreme Allied Commander were a liability when he attempted to direct the land campaign in France himself. He tended to seek the opinions of his principal field commanders, the Englishman, Montgomery, and the Americans, Bradley and Patton, and to work out the best compromise. This was difficult at best because Montgomery and Bradley not only did not

---

[5] Arthur Bryant, *Triumph in the West, 1943–1946,* based on the diaries and autobiographical notes of Field Marshal the Viscount Alanbrooke (London: Collins, 1959), p. 10.

[6] Davis, *Soldier of Democracy,* p. 336.

like each other but also had completely different notions of strategy. Too often Eisenhower sought to integrate his generals into a single strategic plan and succeeded only in falling between stools as a result.[7] For example, in the late summer and early fall of 1944 he promised Montgomery that he would give full support to his army group for an all-out offensive against the Ruhr Basin, the heart of German industrial power. But he then failed to divert the necessary resources to Montgomery to make the action a success because of his reluctance to deny Bradley and Patton supplies on which they insisted. The conciliating genius that was his greatness gave him too great an inclination to compromise in the hard decisions of field operations. Many authorities have felt that what was needed was a commander in chief who possessed a strategy of his own and had the strength to impose it on his commanders without regard for personalities and public opinion.

If Eisenhower were weak in fluid situations in which he felt torn in several directions, he was exceptionally strong in crisis when he could serve as the rallying point for discouragement and low morale. This was particularly true in defensive fighting. For example, he opened the conference at Verdun, which was called to confront the 1944 German winter offensive, with the remark that "there will be only cheerful faces at this conference table."[8] He reacted to the threat more quickly and with more flexibility than any other allied commander and gave the necessary orders for troop transfers and dispersions that enabled the battle to finally be won.

Of course there were situational reasons for his mediating style of leadership as Supreme Allied Commander. He was inexperienced as a strategist and thus tended to defer to his more experienced and more talented field commanders. There were public relations problems in restraining either American or British generals in favor of the other, and the domestic press in both countries was quick to raise a cry about it. American army doctrine called for minimum restraint on field commanders. Eisenhower adhered to the American strategy of a broad front, which permitted the full use of all army groups at all times with few restraints on any. He was an organizer, not a commander, and it was out of character for him to be anything else. Does this leave any room for his personality as a factor in his style

---

[7] Chester Wilmot, *The Struggle for Europe* (London: Collins, 1954), pp. 482–497.
[8] Bryant, *Triumph in the West,* p. 274.

of leadership? It does when we consider that he was originally chosen for the role of Supreme Allied Commander because he had the qualities of an organizer and mediator, not because he was a great strategist. The role he had to play was congenial to the predispositions of his personality.

Two themes run through Eisenhower's style of leadership: voluntarism and order. Voluntarism was embodied by the leader holding himself in restraint, pointing the way to agreement but working primarily out of a collegial concept of organization. Order was exemplified by the search for regularity, coherence, the preconceived plan to inform action, and the common denominator of policy.

Personality Needs

Eisenhower once wrote in criticism of "a too obvious avidity for public acclaim and the delusion that strength of purpose demands arrogant and even insufferable behavior. A soldier once remarked that a man sure of his footing does not need to mount a high horse." [9] In a sense Ike was too healthy to want power over other men. He did not need to mount a high horse because he was sure of his footing. He would never feel that victory in a struggle for influence was a vindication of identity or self-esteem. Lacking the drive for power he never saw it as "personal," but rather as institutional, that is, outside himself.

He knew his strong points to be his likability and gift of inspiring confidence and trust. The bases of his positive leadership style were his disinclination to dominate and his capacity to persuade with charm, empathy, humility, and self-confidence. His strongest need was to like and be liked.

Mental Traits

Eisenhower sought logic and coherence in organization. This was the quality of his mind as well as of his army experience. He sought to structure decisions in such a way that balance and judgment would be emphasized and flux and emotion and conflict minimized. He needed time and regular procedures in order to get a conceptual grasp on problems and develop general guiding formulae.

---

[9] Dwight D. Eisenhower, *Crusade in Europe* (New York: Doubleday and Co., 1948), p. 75.

Values and Ideology

The River Brethren were of the tradition of "Free Soul Protestants." They were committed to the freedom of the inner man and to his autonomy and inner integrity. It was wrong to tamper with that inner preserve. This tradition shaped Eisenhower's voluntarism. He was always reluctant to discipline, to manipulate, to coerce, or to dominate.

The political subculture of his childhood was a frontier environment that exalted individualism, economic materialism as a "spiritual" value, and distrusted the power of government. Like Taft and Hoover, he adhered to a vague orthodoxy of "the American way," which caused an ideological rigidity at times. This subculture, as well as his religious background, demanded a politics of personal rectitude. As President, Eisenhower put great emphasis on the importance of unselfish motives on the part of himself and his associates. He said over and over again that good government was good people. Acts of manipulation that might violate the voluntarism of others or the rectitude of the leader were anathema to him.

His years of staff work in the army shaped a distinctive style out of these elements. He was a diplomat, organizer, and unifier. His experience as Supreme Allied Commander gave him the opportunity to perfect this style, and his success convinced him of the validity of his techniques of leadership.

Conception of the Presidency

Eisenhower enjoyed being President, but he did not seek the office as a vehicle of personal power. Originally, he hoped to be a one-term President who would organize an administration around correct policy goals, and then retire. He saw himself as a reigning monarch who could preside over the nation as a non-partisan figure of national unity and restore government to its proper functions.

Much of his political style followed from this conception. He kept on his desk a block that read, in Latin, "Gentle in manner, strongly in deed." He felt that the best way to lead was, not to seek to manipulate or coerce others, but ". . . a constant seeking for a high and strong ground on which to work together . . . have the diversities brought together in a common purpose, so fair, so reasonable and so appealing that all can rally to it. . . . Only a leadership that is based on honesty of purpose, calmness and inexhaustible patience in conference and persuasion and refusal to be diverted from basic principles can, in the long run, win out. . . . we must never lose sight of the ultimate objective we are trying to attain." [10]

He went into the White House with a belief that F. D. R. had usurped many functions of Congress and that it was his role to restore the balance. This theory was a blend of Republican opinions and his experience from living in Washington in the 1930's. His brother Milton remembered that Ike had worried about Roosevelt's executive dominance. Eisenhower had been one of the first army liason officers on Capitol Hill and he and his chief legislative liason man, former General Jerry Persons, seem to have both retained an old deference for Congress.

His conception of the Presidency was a natural extension of his wartime experience as Supreme Allied Commander and his political values. As Chief of Staff of the army for a brief time after the war he had felt miserable at the political games that his job seemed to involve. It is not surprising that he sought to avoid a "political" dimension to his Presidency.

Leader of Public Opinion

Eisenhower was probably the most popular President of modern times and enjoyed greater freedom from criticism than any other modern President. The bases of this popularity were probably several, although we can only speculate:

(1) With his open, democratic, boyish personality he was an American prototype, a Tom Sawyer grown up.

(2) He was a father figure who inspired confidence. During the war Ernie Pyle had written that if he could pick another father he would pick Ike. The G.I.'s felt this way and so did the American people.

(3) He appealed to the public as a strong man who would bring strength to the government and to world problems.

(4) He appealed to the people as a man of peace who would bring national unity and heal deep, open divisions.

Press Relations

During the war he had enjoyed friendly relations with the working press because he was able to take war correspondents into his con-

---

[10] Dwight D. Eisenhower, *Mandate for Change: The White House Years 1953–1956* (New York: Doubleday and Co., 1963), p. 193.

fidence, make them members of his team, and meet with them in friendly background conferences. This changed when he became a Presidential candidate. He was heard to complain in 1952 about reporters, saying that "some of these guys aren't reporters at all . . . they sound more like district attorneys." [11] His first intention as President was not to hold press conferences and to exclude reporters from the White House proper so that they might not talk to his visitors. His astute press secretary, James Hagerty, persuaded him otherwise, and he held regular conferences, although much less frequently than his predecessors.

Evidently the President-reporter relationship was not very important to him. His non-partisan position and great popularity made him immune to either political or journalistic criticism and newsmen had little choice but to treat him with kid gloves.

The increasing institutionalization of the press conference has made it impossible for the President to give reporters the same kind of background and off-the-record information in the press conference itself as some previous Presidents had been able to give. Held in a lecture room and covered by television cameras, the press conferences provided increasingly less opportunity for repartee between the President and the press. Because the President's words appeared verbatim in the transcript of the conference, he had to be much more careful in what he said. This cannot be blamed on Eisenhower, for these developments began with Truman. However, Eisenhower's political personality was well suited to this kind of superficial coverage. Although he answered every question put to him, he seldom answered with color or impact. This did not seem to hurt him with the public. The public looked for the image of the man they liked and admired rather than to the content of what he said. Some observers felt that his frequent lack of information about matters and his unprofessional replies, which made further questioning useless, sustained his image as a sincere man, doing his best.

Cornwell concludes that Eisenhower made a very limited use of press conferences for leading Congress or the nation. He displayed greater willingness than F. D. R. to discuss and endorse pending bills, however, but this was seldom part of a strategy of leadership. Cornwell found little evidence of timing of statements in relation to public events or Congressional acts. The President permitted reporters to set the content of the conferences by responding passively to their ques-

[11] Cornwell, *Presidential Leadership*, p. 177.

tions, and he seldom tried to guide the meetings. On the other hand, on matters about which he felt a moral fervor, especially fiscal responsibility, he could be forceful and persistent in his remarks in the press conference. Cornwell concludes that the Eisenhower record of using press conferences to lead opinion was "a curious mixture of rigorous advocacy on some topics with an essentially passive approach on others." [12] What was lacking was a sense of political strategy.

Eisenhower was often said to be a genius at public relations who built up his extraordinary public image between 1941 and 1952. This was not so. The American press made him a folk hero during the war because of his position and his glowing personality. However, he did not like this publicity and he deliberately played himself down during the war. As President he was no different. He insisted on believing that it was his ideals that had made him popular rather than his person. He disliked making speeches, appearing before crowds, and had little skill or taste for the manipulation of media in his own behalf. [13] He was much like Hoover in this regard, except that, unlike Hoover, he had a warm, expansive personality, which could be dramatized, and a skillful press secretary, James Hagerty, who knew how to do the job. Ike was happy to leave news details and strategy to Hagerty, who was the President's only link with reporters. The President refused to have background conferences with reporters and Hagerty and other administration officials played this role. Most observers felt Hagerty to be more a press agent than a secretary for his efforts were expended toward making his chief look good. But, as Cornwell points out, this was occasioned not so much by Hagerty's activity as by Eisenhower's near abdication of a public relations role.

For an illustration of Eisenhower's lack of sensitivity to his power stakes as they were shaped by his public statements, we can look at the Little Rock school integration crisis of 1957. In July, 1957, the President told a news conference that he could not imagine any set of circumstances that would induce him to send federal troops into any area to enforce the order of a federal court. The common sense of America would never require it, he said. [14] This statement gave an unintended green light to Governor Orval Faubus to act to defy the federal court without sanction from Washington. This was precisely

[12] Cornwell, *Presidential Leadership*, pp. 177–182.
[13] Cornwell, *Presidential Leadership*, p. 218.
[14] Emmet John Hughes, *The Ordeal of Power: A Political Memoir of the Eisenhower Years* (New York: Atheneum, 1963), p. 243.

what he did in September. Eisenhower's lack of artistry here was surely a contributing factor to the Little Rock crisis.

Eisenhower's speech writers gave Cornwell different accounts of how deeply involved the President was in the preparation of speeches. Evidently, his interest was sporadic. Hughes insisted that "his greatest aversion was the calculated rhetorical device. This meant more than a healthy scorn for the contrived and effortful. It extended to a distrust of eloquence, of resonance, sometimes even of simple effectiveness of expression." [15]

Ike was committed to a strategy of leadership that emphasized good will, the rationality of publics and leaders, and himself as a source of unity. Therefore, he avoided emotional appeals and emphasized and appealed to national unity with himself as the symbol of unity. This was not political artistry in terms of policy leadership, but it was amazingly effective unconscious artistry in terms of the non-political foundation of his own popularity. I say unconscious because his popularity seems to have come to him without effort or skill on his part.

Legislative Leader

In a 1956 press conference Eisenhower was asked if he intended to use sanctions against Republican legislators who had voted against his programs. His response was characteristic: "I am not one of the desk-pounding type that likes to stick out his jaw and look like he is bossing the show." [16] For him it was either a case of persuasion on the basis of reason and morality or naked domination, and he preferred the former.

He put principal reliance on his persuasive powers and his good will. His personality was to be the bridge to agreement. One of his favorite stories was of Lincoln calling on General McClellan at his home. McClellan, who was out, knew that Lincoln was there but did not deign to return home. Lincoln was heard to comment that he would wait all night, if necessary, if it would help win the war. Eisenhower, like Lincoln in this instance, saw the qualities of self-abnegation and patience as the marks of a true leader. What counted was not his own glorification but the furtherance of ideals.

[15] Cornwell, *Presidential Leadership,* p. 292.
[16] Binkley, *President and Congress,* p. 354.

Eisenhower ran for the Presidency in 1952 as a "moderate" Republican pledged to active American involvement in international affairs and acceptance of mild social reform at home. He had been nominated over the opposition of the conservative wing of his party, but this wing held the positions of Congressional leadership. His opponent for the nomination, Robert A. Taft, was the Senate majority leader. The President thus faced the same dilemma that Taft and Hoover had faced, and his response, like theirs, was to seek close ties with the leadership. However, like Taft and Hoover, he lacked the skill and staying power to take the initiative and keep it. Also, like Taft and Hoover, his own ideas of a "moderate" policy were a source of weakness for his resolution as a legislative leader. Throughout his administration Eisenhower vacillated, in domestic policies, between a reform and a conservative position. He could not come to firm agreement with himself on questions of civil rights, federal aid to education, and government spending. This was a handicap to his capacities for leadership because it soon became clear in Washington that he was not prepared to go to the mat for many of his policies.

His initial problem in his first two years was that members of his own party in Congress were his worst enemies. Senator Joseph McCarthy kept looking for Communists in a Republican administration. Senator William Knowland, who replaced Taft as Senate majority leader upon the latter's death, was in continuous disagreement with the President. Senator Bricker attempted to deprive the executive branch of its treaty-making power by the Bricker amendment.

Eisenhower's response was patience, persuasion, continuous consultation, and private fuming about "those monkeys" on the Hill. He relied on his own good will to bring them around and refused to use either the sanctions of patronage or appeal to public opinion to bring them into line. It is not possible to attack Congress and conciliate it at the same time, he reasoned to aides. But once he confessed in a moment of gloom that "I don't know any other way to lead." [17]

The principal legislative incidents of his first two years were those in which he was forced to fight defensively against members of his own party in Congress. An example of the kind of irresolution and ineptness that beset his efforts to conciliate can be seen in the fight over the Bricker amendment.

[17] Hughes, *The Ordeal of Power*, p. 123.

During the fight, the President told his Cabinet that he was anxious simultaneously to protect Presidential prerogatives and to relieve the legitimate fears of those supporting the amendment. Those fears were that a treaty might someday be used to contravene United States law. He said he believed the amendment would be beaten but he took pride in how the administration had been decent and reasonable in the controversy without surrendering on any essential points.[18] That was not quite the whole story. The President had been anxious to conciliate Bricker, and had given the Senator friendly hearings in the White House on the matter. Evidently the warm and friendly tone of the talks gave Bricker the false impression that Eisenhower was more willing to compromise than was actually the case. The President did tell Bricker that he would accept the amendment if a key clause were eliminated. However, at the same time, Secretary of State Dulles had told Republican senators supporting the President that no part of the amendment was acceptable. This seemed to place Eisenhower in an inconsistent position. At a subsequent Cabinet meeting, Dulles was critical of administration policy as fuzzy. The President defended himself as having told Bricker he would go only so far and no further, at which Dulles is said to have retorted: "I know, Sir, but you haven't told any one else." [19] Eventually, when Bricker refused to compromise, the President became disgusted and sent Senator Knowland a letter opposing the amendment. This firm stand resulted in its defeat by a small margin. Had Bricker been willing to compromise, the President might have been drawn into support of an unwise amendment in his anxiety to conciliate.

The running feud of Senator McCarthy with the administration probably did more to damage the President's professional reputation than any other single series of events. McCarthy, using his investigating committee, ran riot through the administration, investigating the U.S.I.A., hurling charges at the State Department, and finally attacking the army for harboring Communists. Eisenhower adhered to his practice of not discussing personalities and, while he privately fumed, he told aides, "I will not get into the gutter with that guy." He resolved to let McCarthy hang himself, which eventually happened, culminating in the Senate censure of the Wisconsin Senator. But Eisen-

[18] Robert J. Donovan, *Eisenhower: The Inside Story* (New York: Harper & Row, 1956), p. 240.

[19] Sherman Adams, *Firsthand Report* (New York: Harper and Row, 1961), p. 106; and Hughes, *The Ordeal of Power,* p. 144.

hower had little to do with the final comeuppance. Sherman Adams felt that all along the President had had no strategy for handling McCarthy except a desire to ignore him.[20]

It is not easy to say what Eisenhower might have done to bring Republican leaders more into line in the beginning. His failure to do so, however, was probably a factor in the Republican loss of Congress in 1954. Many critics have suggested that had he taken a stronger line from the beginning, made more frequent appeals to the public, used patronage skillfully, and refused to place himself in compromising situations with men who were hostile to him, the story might have been different. We cannot discuss what might have been. What is clear is that, being the kind of man he was, Ike could not have acted other than he did.

There can be no doubt that sometimes this strategy had positive results. By persistent courting Eisenhower enlisted the loyal support of Senator Taft, whose defection might have been disastrous. In the process Taft did many things for the President he might not have done on his own. The President succeeded in getting rank and file support among Congressional Republicans to the degree that substantial portions of his programs passed in 1953 and 1954. This was part of a gradual process in which Eisenhower created by deliberate intent a new mood in the nation, a mood of unity and peace after the harsh years of domestic conflict in the Truman administration. It was congenial to the average Republican member of Congress to reflect and support this mood and support the President's moderate program.

Tactical Weakness

Ike was weak in fluid situations where he was pulled in more than one way. As during the war, he tended to fall between stools. There were several reasons for this. He usually tried to please too many people. His logical, orderly mind was not quick to react in fast moving, unstructured situations. He lacked a sense of personal power in the Presidency. He was of many minds about much of his own legislative program and permitted his irresolution to weaken his public posture.

In early 1957 the Secretary of the Treasury, George Humphrey, read the Cabinet a letter he intended to send to the President about the new budget. In it he said that the budget had still not been cut enough. The Director of the Bureau of the Budget, Percival F. Brund-

---

[20] Donovan, *The Inside Story,* p. 257.

age, thought it would be taken as a sign of a rift within the administration. The President sided with Humphrey, reasoning that it might help discourage Congress from increasing expenditures even more. When reporters asked the President about the Secretary's comments, he not only supported Humphrey but also invited Congress to cut his budget in any way that they felt it could reasonably be cut. He seemed to repudiate his own budget. His argument was that the President shares the budgetary power with Congress and would appreciate Congressional advice in the matter. Republican leaders in Congress were confused and angry.

How could the administration simultaneously defend and yet urge the cutting of its budget, they asked? The Eisenhower-Humphrey answer was that Congress should cut the budget in areas where Congress had authorized spending, such as rivers and harbors. This was not realistic, to say the least. The House, in a playful mood, passed a resolution asking the President to tell Congress where to cut expenditures and Senate majority leader Johnson made a public plea for Presidential guidance in the matter.

Eisenhower's indecision seems to have been due to increasing concern about the high rate of federal spending. However, he did not protect or channel this concern with any sense of the artistry of power. He supported Humphrey without thinking that he had anything to lose. He thought of himself as only one man on a team that shared authority with Congress and not as the central actor in a drama, whom all the other actors were watching.

The aftermath was that Congress began to cut into foreign aid funds, and the President had to spend the spring fighting for his mutual security program. He finally had to resort to a television appeal to the public. In August he had to accept a reduced foreign aid program and did so with great disappointment, regarding it as a personal defeat.[21]

A similar instance occurred that summer when he revealed at a news conference that he did not understand his own civil rights bill then in Congress. He said that he was not clear about a certain provision and intended to ask the Attorney General about it. At his next meeting with reporters he disclosed that he disagreed with a provision of his own bill. This doubt and indecision on the part of the President were disheartening to those in Congress of both parties who sought passage of the bill. He had played into the hands of Southern senators. Finally, after coaching, he told reporters where he stood on

[21] Adams, *Firsthand Report,* pp. 366–380.

the bill, but, despite his attempts, the jury trial amendment, which the Attorney General opposed, was adopted by the Senate. Eisenhower told the Cabinet it was one of his most serious political defeats. As usual, he attributed no responsibility to himself for that defeat.

Again, scepticism about the substance of the bill was at the root of his vacillation. And, again, his lack of artistry was responsible for the manner of his vacillation.[22]

In 1958 the President presented his personal plan for the further unification of the Defense Department to Congress. It was a matter about which he felt strongly. He wrote most of the legislation himself, an unusual thing for a President to do, and he told reporters, when they suggested that there would be Congressional opposition, that he did not care how strong or how numerous it was; he had more military experience in directing unified forces than anyone on active duty.[23] Clearly, here was a man determined to fight. He sent the plan to Congress with a strong message calling for enactment. It was assumed in Congress that he was taking an unshakable and uncompromising stand on it.

But then he failed to follow through. He told a news conference that he did not consider the language of the bill sacrosanct, and added that, since he would only be Commander in Chief for three more years, his "personal convictions, no matter how strong," could not be the final answer.[24] After that, Secretary of Defense McElroy was trapped by the chairman of the House Armed Services Committee into admitting that certain provisions of the bill were not needed. These two things were all that the chairman, who opposed the bill, needed, and in good time the bill was seriously weakened. A last-minute statement by the President made no difference.

Standing Up to Congress

He was a better defensive than offensive fighter. This quality came to the fore even more after the Democrats took control of Congress in 1955. Many times during the remaining years Eisenhower was to score victories over the Democratic leadership and to thwart their designs on him by simple defensive tactics, such as the judicious use of the veto power. This was not really a new Eisenhower. It was the

[22] Adams, *Firsthand Report,* pp. 341, 342.
[23] Adams, *Firsthand Report,* p. 418.
[24] Marquis Childs, *Eisenhower: The Captive Hero* (New York: Harcourt, Brace and World, 1958), p. 270.

man in a more congenial role, that of, as he often said in conversation, "refusing to be stampeded."

Throughout his tenure he gave sporadic bursts of positive leadership of Congress, but they were uneven and unpredictable, and not part of any over-all strategy. He was more effective on the defensive. He used the veto power, against a 1956 agricultural act that was tailored for the election, against pork barrel rivers and harbors measures, and he publicly threatened to veto many other measures and thus stopped them dead. Likewise, he exerted positive leadership in several areas, his highway program, the mutual security program, which was a running fight every year, reciprocal trade programs, and so forth. His greatest period of strength *vis-à-vis* Congress was in the period when theoretically, as a lame duck, he should have been the weakest, his last two sessions of 1959 and 1960. In those sessions he was wholly on the defensive, and, as Neustadt points out, he was on the strongest ground a lame duck President can be on, the ground of opposition to Congressional initiative when Congress does not bear his party's label.[25] He launched a crusade to defend his budgets against Congressional attempts to add to them, and his weapon was the selective veto and threat of the veto. As Neustadt points out, Eisenhower was consistently opposing measures that he had once advocated in his own programs but had not given wholehearted support. His new strength was that he knew his own mind. During this period he went beyond the use of the veto and used other traditional weapons, the press conference, public statements, personal appeals to public opinion, and personal communications to Congressional leaders. Here he was fighting for a basic tenet of his entire tenure, fiscal responsibility. The issue was clear-cut, the villians—Democratic spenders—were in the open. He forced them to tailor their proposals to his wishes.

During this period it was common for newspapermen and columnists to write that the President was finally coming into his own as a strong President; he was beginning to understand and enjoy the Presidential prerogatives. This was going too far. It is true that he told associates that he was going to do nothing to weaken the Presidential office, and that he enjoyed the victories over the opposition. But this was not a new Eisenhower. It was the old Eisenhower refusing to be stampeded. This Eisenhower could not have pursued a vigorous offensive drive against Congress because that was not his stock in

---

[25] Neustadt, *Presidential Power,* p. 85.

trade. Therefore, to show that he was not a weak President in terms of self-defense is not to show that he was a strong President in terms of offense or tactical skill.

Administrative Leader

In January of 1956 the President was asked by a reporter about his running for reelection. He replied that he would find it necessary to isolate himself from pressures in order to reach a logical decision.[26] This answer told much about his style of decision-making. Sherman Adams remembered that in the summer of 1954 he felt that Eisenhower's spells of depression were due to the many vexing problems that either had no solution or that required great personal concentration before making decisions for which the President alone was responsible.[27]

Eisenhower's administrative style in the White House was that which he had developed and tested as Supreme Allied Commander. The purpose of personal staff was to free the leader from the pressure of details not relevant for major decisions. The leader had to break free to think and work in peace. As in the army, he sought to make the organization beneath him as much a single mind as possible. This result was to be ensured by putting the right men in the right posts and ensuring negotiation all along the chain of command so that most conflicts could be resolved and only the most acute problems would rise to the top. The role of the leader in this organization was to provide a spirit of unity and guiding ideals and settle major decisions that were pushed up to him.[28]

Eisenhower revived the Cabinet meeting as a regular occurrence. It fitted with his desire for well-prepared, collective discussion with himself thinking out loud and making the final decision at the meeting. One of his purposes was to promote Administration solidarity by ensuring consensus. He remembered the disunity of the Roosevelt administration with horror and condemned Roosevelt's practice of making all the decisions himself.[29] This type of meeting followed logically from Eisenhower's willingness to delegate much policy-making authority to his department heads and wait until it was fully

[26] Adams, *Firsthand Report,* p. 228.
[27] Adams, *Firsthand Report,* p. 128.
[28] Fenno, *The President's Cabinet,* pp. 108–148.
[29] Eisenhower, *Mandate,* p. 134.

worked out before listening to them. He had a strong reaction against policies presented to him without prior thought or interdepartmental consultation. It reflected his desire to educate himself through a focused discussion.

The President preferred to thrash out difficult domestic questions with the whole Cabinet present rather than see individual department heads about such problems in his office. There is a paradox here. While he deliberately sought a clash of views in Cabinet meetings, it is much more likely in group meetings of this kind that conflicts will be muted and transferred by those involved to other arenas where the compulsion to agree is less operative. Thus, it is likely that the President might have gotten more accurate pictures of the views and disagreements among his department heads if he had dealt with each privately and taken a greater part in personally deciding between such disputes. But this was not his way.

He gave his individual department heads great latitude in policy formation and almost always backed them up publicly even when they made bad mistakes. He seemed content to set general guidelines of policy and let each of his associates develop and apply those guidelines. It sometimes seemed in the process as if the original policy themes were bent considerably and as if department heads were going in different directions in overlapping policy areas, with a confused President acting as referee between them.

One example of the loose control that the President held over his associates came in the spring of 1953 when Attorney General Brownell informed the President he was going to make a speech attacking former President Truman for disregarding F.B.I. files indicating that a Presidential appointee was a Communist. This was the famous Harry Dexter White case. Brownell's motives have never been disclosed but it was widely thought he was trying to steal the thunder of Senator McCarthy, who at the time was busy attacking the administration. The President told Brownell that it was his responsibility as a responsible government official to act and he would back him up. Later, at a press conference, he admitted that at the time he had been unclear as to who White was. He had relied on Brownell's judgment, he said. The criticism against Brownell after the speech was made was for the use of secret F.B.I. files in a political attack. The President was on the hot spot because, after the fact, he was obviously sorry the dispute had developed but he could not fail to support Brownell. This episode was sheer ineptness on Eisenhower's part rather than calculation, for at the time he was very anxious for Democratic Congressional support against attacks of his own party leaders, and he had cause to regret the Brownell attack.[30]

There was a reverse side to Eisenhower's disengagement from his own administration. He retained a balance and judgment that permitted him to overrule his top associates and keep his administration on a steady course whenever it became necessary to do so. Just as he did not participate in many of their positive initiatives, so did he not permit himself to be taken in by many of their ideas and suggestions. This was especially true in foreign and military matters. As in other areas of government, he refused to be "stampeded," but marched to his own beat. One example was his resistance to Pentagon advice for American military action in French Indo-China at the moment of French defeat.

During the Suez crisis in 1956 before he was to speak to the nation, he went out to hit golf balls on the White House lawn. His speech writer remembered feeling resentment that the President was relaxing while speech was being written. But the later impression of firmness and moderation created by the speech caused him to realize that this was Eisenhower's talent, to stay calm while others were panicking.[31] This was the reason that the President continually sought to get away from Washington, to get onto the golf course, to isolate himself from pressures, to compose his thoughts. Merriman Smith, the White House United Press correspondent, felt that the President had a safety valve in him that told him when it was time to quit work and relax or else he would explode.[32] This had its bad side; it explains the peculiar passivity, as for example during the Little Rock crisis, when he took a long time before standing up to Governor Faubus, but it also explains the balance and judgment that went into his handling of other crises. This was the inner strength that permitted him to tolerate McCarthy, to be permissive toward Congress, and to restrain himself in so many ways. Often, when he did not act, he was being most decisive.

Neustadt and Rossiter agree that Eisenhower's great contribution to the Presidency was his organization of the White House staff so that it freed the President from petty details and gave him the gift of time. What he did with his time was another matter. Rossiter felt that he

[30] Adams, *Firsthand Report,* p. 138.
[31] Hughes, *The Ordeal of Power,* p. 220.
[32] Merriman Smith, *Meet Mr. Eisenhower* (New York: Harper and Row, 1955), p. 226.

wasted it on the golf course. Neustadt believes that he failed to use it to increase his sources of information outside of that available to him through official channels.[33] It was not the staff system or the apparatus of collegial government in the Cabinet and the NSC that scholars have criticized but rather the use Eisenhower made of these institutions. I want to sum up the general criticisms below:

1. He was weak in the gathering of information outside of official channels and therefore often denied himself the kind of information about personalities and conflicts within his administration that might have increased his effectiveness. Often, he was the last man in the chain of command to know of things.[34]

2. He was weak in implementing his own policy once it had been formulated. He assumed that, as in the army, policy would automatically be translated into action down the chain of command. In actual fact, this is not so. For example, he was continuously frustrated at the inability of his administration to formulate coherent disarmament proposals but he could find no effective way of breaking the vicious circle of disagreements among the Pentagon, the A.E.C., and the State Department.[35] His reluctance to intervene personally in lower echelons was perhaps a handicap.

3. He failed to use conflicts within his administration to encourage creativity and spontaneity. This may help explain the poverty of ideas of which he himself often complained.[36]

4. He permitted himself to become a voluntary prisoner of his White House staff. Sherman Adams was an assistant president for six years under Eisenhower. He, not the President, supervised the White House staff. He was the President's principal source of information on domestic administrative matters. As he relates in his memoirs, Adams's passion was to protect Eisenhower from minor problems, conflicts, and details, so that he might be freed for the great decisions of state. The President often said that Adams understood his purposes better than any one man. There is no evidence that Adams usurped Presidential prerogatives. He was self-effacing and loyal.

However, Adams, and the notion of a chief of staff in the White House, came under the criticism that the President was being denied

[33] Rossiter, *The American Presidency,* pp. 167–170; Neustadt, *Presidential Power,* p. 146.

[34] Hughes, *The Ordeal of Power,* p. 152.

[35] Adams, *Firsthand Report,* p. 112.

[36] Neustadt, *Presidential Power,* p. 153; Feno, *The President's Cabinet,* p. 111.

information essential to his tasks. For example, Senator John Sherman Cooper tried and failed repeatedly to see the President to warn him of the political danger of the Dixon-Yates contract by which a private power company was to build a plant for the T.V.A. Dixon-Yates later flared up as a major issue. But the President was not interested in this kind of information.[37] He did not shape his actions by such considerations. There is no evidence that the White House Staff ever denied the President any major pieces of knowledge.

It was falsely assumed that the President was a prisoner of his staff. This is not very likely. No President can be a prisoner of his staff unless he chooses to be. Eisenhower was not a prisoner. He simply wanted his staff to handle a good many things that held no interest for him. He did not have any special love for the political process or the administrative jungle as challenges for Presidential skills. He wanted to be free for the big decisions.

It would not be fair to criticize Eisenhower because he was not the freewheeling executive that F.D.R. had been. The federal establishment could not be run in that fashion any longer. It was too large and complex, and ridden with crisis. In this sense Eisenhower brought a much needed order and system to Presidential decision-making and the organization of the executive branch. However, he did not work at maximizing Presidential power within this new bureaucratic framework. Army experience, his concept of collegial government, his mental processes, his disinclination to work as hard as he might, and his insensitivity to power conflicts all handicapped his power sense.

Conclusion

The same pattern presents itself over and over again in Eisenhower's career. He was a strong organizer, coordinator, and conciliator. These skills were rooted in his easy rapport with others, his drive to impose order on the world, his voluntarist values, and his military experience. His greatest success came when his personality and abilities fitted the requirements of the wartime Allied command. However, even then there were portents that he was not a strategic leader, but was rather a mediator. Wartime experiences showed him to be at his weakest in fluid situations where he had to choose quickly between alternatives.

He showed the same strengths and weaknesses as President, and in

[37] Marquis Childs, *Eisenhower: The Captive Hero,* p. 227.

politics as well as soldiering his lack of strategic sense and weakness in fluid situations was a great handicap. He brought order and unity to the government and created a moderate political climate but he lacked the political skills to lead in the Presidency. The great paradox about Eisenhower was that he was a strong man who deliberately avoided many techniques of leadership because of his personality, mentality, and values.

CONCLUSION:

Personality and the Presidency

> *. . . there exists the closest of connections between self-help in the Presidency and three aspects of a President's interior resources: his power sense, his confidence—which turns on his self-image—and his sense of direction.*[1]

WE HAVE COMPARED six Presidents in terms of a model of political personality and a model of Presidential roles. We have postulated norms of skill for each role and asked how personality contributed to skill. By itself a static model will not tell us about dynamic relationships. But by joining the two models we can draw out propositions about personality and skill. The number of cases reinforces the propositions if the relationships are repeated in more than one case.

These models are put forward as frameworks for the analysis of past, and perhaps present, Presidents. They may not help to predict how men will behave in office in the future. Any predictive value of our propositions is very general. They suggest the kinds of skills to expect in certain kinds of men. Perhaps political scientists can use biographical and historical case studies on a wide comparative scale to say more about the interaction of personalities, institutions, and culture. Our concern here is to say a few things about the Presidency.

Personality, Skill, and Roles

Our six subjects have been grouped into two "types," which are only labels for a number of characteristics shared by those in each grouping. Obviously all past and future Presidents will not fall within each of these types. These are relatively pure types in the Presidency. They seem to reflect strong tendencies in American political culture. But we can compare these, and other, Presidents in terms of needs, mental traits, values, and skills, and assess the consequences of different kinds of personality for the office.

---

[1] Neustadt, *Presidential Power*, p. 163.

1. LEADERSHIP OF PUBLIC OPINION. The Presidents of Action were skillful in this role. The two Roosevelts developed dramatizing skills in initial response to the need for attention. These skills were first developed in private life and then used in politics. They had great intuitive sensitivity as to how to get and keep the attention of others in the playing of political roles. Certainly the way in which they led public opinion reflected this sensitivity. This need was the root of their great empathy for the thoughts and moods of others, which was a staple in their political style. Wilson did not seem to have the need for self-advertisement and his political style reflected this fact. His technical skill at leading public opinion was rooted in his drive for power over the minds of men and he developed oratorical skill in response to this imperative. But his was not a dramatizing style.

Skill in leading public opinion in all three men was also a function of their larger sense of political leadership. Their conception of the Presidency and their sense of purpose in their programs were also important factors. Needs for attention and power were likewise a part of this larger set of motivations.

The Presidents of Restraint did not have the technical skills that we value in leading public opinion because none had the needs that stimulate such skills. If anything, their personalities would not permit self-dramatization. None of their pre-Presidential training encouraged them to develop such skills. Their values also were a handicap. They deprecated drama, emotion in politics, and tricks and manipulations.

Eisenhower is a possible exception to this. He was personable and popular and liked to show himself to crowds. This reflected his general liking for people and his desire to be liked. But he seems to have underestimated his ability to move people in large numbers and to have felt uncomfortable as a popular hero. His needs did not drive him to dramatize himself.

However, more important for him as well as for Taft and Hoover is the fact that none of them had very well-developed strategic ideas about how to lead public opinion. Their conception of the Presidency, their distrust of many techniques of leadership, and their resistance to popular reform suggests that this kind of President finds it most congenial to be a symbolic leader above the political strife. The hard tasks of political leadership would seem to be more congenial to those leaders who are initially propelled to win public acceptance of themselves as persons. In them this search becomes part of the fight to win acceptance for policy. In both cases, the larger conception of leadership complements needs.

2. LEGISLATIVE LEADERSHIP.   The Presidents of Action possessed technical skill in leading Congress. This skill was initially rooted in their needs for personal power. Over the years, and especially in their early careers, they developed abilities that served this need. This emotional imperative can be seen as a consistent undercurrent in their legislative leadership. It was an extra incentive.

The need for power had a different quality in each case. The two Roosevelts were perhaps not so driven as Wilson and therefore they could enjoy the process of leading for its own sake without having to feel that they must win every fight. They were capable of greater flexibility than Wilson. In this sense they were more fitted for the demands of Presidential legislative leadership. Wilson's inner demands were too rigid at times. He could lead Congress effectively only in certain kinds of situations. This suggests that the need for personal power, although necessary to skill, can be so intense that it becomes self-defeating. It may be that the kind of personality seen in modern dictators such as Hitler cannot rise to the top in stable democracies. Their demands for power are too intense.

The strategic skill of the Presidents of Action was rooted in the drive for personal power, but also in their conceptions of Presidential leadership, their sense of purpose, and their experience in developing strategies by which to lead others. Needs supplied the technical skill but not the larger sense of strategy and purpose. Their values reinforced their skills. They saw themselves as midwives of history. The fact that other men accepted this as true helps to explain their success but the certainty itself was a factor in their sense of efficacy and thus in their skill.

The Presidents of Restraint were not driven by the need for personal power and therefore lacked the skills that follow from such a need. Not driven by the need for personal power and coming from technical professions, they emphasized reason, appeals to unity, and morality as the means of persuasion and they downgraded manipulative leadership.

Of course their lack of a larger sense of legislative strategy was due to their conception of the Presidency, their deference to Congress, and their desire to be Presidents above the political struggle. They also put less emphasis on dominating Congress because they wanted less government action than the Presidents of Action. Taft and Eisenhower lacked a sure sense of legislative purpose, which weakened their ability to lead. Hoover's sense of purpose was so rigid as to be disabling. It is interesting that the self-defeating qualities in the leadership styles of both Hoover and Wilson seem to have been rooted in similar traits of political personality, their compulsive stubbornness, mental rigidity, and moralism.

3. ADMINISTRATIVE LEADERSHIP.   The drive for personal power of the Presidents of Action informed their sense of Presidential power. As in legislative leadership, the two Roosevelts loved process for its own sake more than Wilson, who was more a prisoner of his need to dominate than they. This was a handicap to him in controlling bureaucracy.

Each of them saw administration as a political dimension, and saw that their control was by no means automatic. Thus, while their need for power gave them a sensitivity to Presidential power, their conception of the Presidency as the center of decision was the dominant and guiding factor in their style of administration.

It is not clear that there was any relationship between their policy ideals and programs and their style of administration.

The lack of need for power in the Presidents of Restraint seems to have dulled their sense of Presidential power. Hoover might seem an exception to this since he was so determined to dominate his administration. But he did not so much want power over persons as authority over organization and mastery of problems. He saw associates and subordinates as means to these ends.

As we have seen in the performance of every Presidential role, for both types, the sensitivity to and need for personal power was only one part of a larger conception of administrative leadership. Conceptions of the Presidency, a dislike of conflict, a technical background, and qualities of intellect all caused these Presidents to fail to see the political dimension of administration.

As with the Presidents of Action, there does not seem to have been any relationship between their policies and programs and their administrative style.

Real consequences follow from the administrative styles of each type of President. The two Roosevelts kept superb control over bureaucracy by treating it as a political area in which the problems of Presidential power were essentially the same as those in other areas. This strategy not only made for control but it also pushed information up to the chief executive and gave him channels by which to implement policy. Taft and Eisenhower did not keep sufficient control over bureaucracy and thus tended to deny themselves needed information and have difficulty implementing policies once they were made. Wilson and Hoover were similar in their type of administration, which was "close to the vest," and both suffered from their unwillingness to delegate authority. This common style was perhaps rooted in their common rigidity of mind and ideology. Wilson was perhaps a less effective administrator than Hoover because of his drive for power. It was almost too intense to be useful.

4. AN IDEAL TYPE OF PRESIDENT? The two Roosevelts came closest to having the kinds of political personalities that can best perform Presidential roles by the criteria that have been advanced. They needed attention and power and these needs shaped their skills of leadership. However, these needs were not so intense as to be self-defeating. They had flexible, empirical minds, which permitted them to be adaptable and resourceful in finding solutions to problems. They seldom strayed too far in their thinking from what the traffic would bear but they were always pushing to go a little beyond that point. Their conceptions of the Presidential office, as a place for political leadership, informed and guided all their efforts. They were "political men" whose image of the Presidency was of themselves in the White House. These men are rare but they are essential to effective Presidential leadership.

We can expect certain consequences for the conduct of the office from such men. They will try to lead the nation in new directions, to educate the public. They will try to dominate Congress, with varying degrees of success, depending upon general political conditions. They will increase bureaucratic vitality and innovation by their catalytic style of administration. In sum, they will serve the principal purpose that a President of Action can serve, of being a catalyst to the national life.

Truman, Kennedy, and Johnson

Our analytic models may help to understand the three most recent Presidents of Action. They have not been treated in full for several reasons. Truman was originally President by accident and would never have normally been in the office. Kennedy was not permitted a full opportunity to develop. Johnson is too recent to be judged. However, a brief look at them in terms of our categories may suggest the utility of this approach. Any propositions suggested are only hypotheses.

Harry S. Truman never wanted to be President and often yearned to return to the Senate. He had none of the psychological needs that we have tied to skill. However, he was a reader of history, an admirer of Wilson and Roosevelt, and he venerated the Presidential office. He had the conception of the Presidency of the two Roosevelts and Wilson without their skills of leadership.

Certain personal qualities reinforced this respect for Presidential power. He loved to make decisions and he was aggressive. Therefore, he organized his administration for the making of decisions and he defended Presidential prerogatives and powers against everyone. He was most successful as an administrator. Although he valued system and organization much as Eisenhower did he was more accessible and fonder of reaching out for information and decisions. Thus he was more on top of his job than was Eisenhower.

However, he did not have Roosevelt's sense of personal power stakes in the administrative process. He had no sense of strategy but made decisions as they came to him without considering their relationship to other decisions. Thus, he often let the initiatives of other men time his decisions and his political strategy suffered because of it.[2]

His manner of leading public opinion was much like his decision-making. He had no sense of grand strategy but took each case as it came. He seldom prepared the public in advance for policy departures. Of course, he had to face more crises than F. D. R., who excelled at such preparation, but Truman's episodic approach to leadership was also responsible.[3]

Cornwell finds that Truman failed to use his press conferences for educating public opinion. He made brief responses to the questions and did not voluntarily add additional information. He approached the conferences as an ordeal. Evidently, the subtle prod of a need for attention was not present in him. The same was true of his use of television. He treated it as an adjunct to radio. Of course, he had had little experience with the projecting of ideas and personality on a national stage and it was too late to learn. It is interesting that the public podium on which he was most at home was the campaign trail.

His leadership of Congress was very uneven. In general, he felt it was his duty to advocate policies in a forthright manner. If Congress did not respond, at least he had done his duty. He had no gift for elaborate legislative strategy. His forthrightness served him well when Congress could be persuaded to act, for example, in the adoption of the Marshall Plan. At times, his combativeness was to his political

---

[2] Neustadt, *Presidential Power,* pp. 163, 164.
[3] Cornwell, *Presidential Leadership,* p. 269.

advantage. He drew much political benefit from his attacks on the Republican 80th Congress. But, at other times, he wrangled and fought with Congress in a petty and unnecessary manner, such as his bypassing of Congress in the decision to go into Korea and the subsequent wrangling about it, or his disregard for Congressional prerogatives in the decision to send troops to Europe. He was simply doing his duty as he saw it, but with a conspicuous lack of skill.

His view of the Presidency fitted his times. The man who liked decisions had many crucial ones to make: to drop the first atomic bomb, to rescue Berlin, to continue nuclear research, to contain Communism in Europe and Asia. He made these decisions squarely and bravely. But, on balance, he cannot be seen as politically skillful. He had half the equipment for Presidential skill, that is, the necessary conception of the office. But he was not a completely "political man" in terms of his needs and drives and his political style revealed this.

John F. Kennedy had drives for action, challenge, and excellence in achievement. He had all the ambitions of the Kennedys. But he does not seem to have had a strong need to influence or win power over others for its own sake. He was primarily interested in meeting and solving problems.

He was a rationalist, who distrusted emotion in politics and liked to apply the yardstick of reason and factual analysis against every proposal. Similarly, he tried to use reason in his persuasion of men.

His values were a blend of the skeptic and the romantic. He was skeptical of popular courage and wisdom and did not expect too much of the political process. Yet, his romantic aspect caused him to love excellence and to preach visions.

His conception of the Presidency was that of past Presidents of Action, but he does not seem to have felt that the fulfillment of the office was himself in the White House. Rather, he saw it simply as a hard but exciting job. He wanted to be in the thick of the action and that was in the White House.

As a leader of public opinion he was not a dramatist. Although he was extremely adept at public relations techniques he seems to have had a deeply rooted disinclination to dramatize himself. He was intellectual in his approach to public opinion and was happier in the cut and thrust of the press conference than he was barnstorming.

He was afraid to carry too many issues to the public because he felt the public mood was against new departures. In this he may have been accurate. However, it is hard to imagine him as a crusader. His gift was to break the ice on many new issues, for example, civil rights and economic questions, in his cool, analytic way. He was a good catalytic leader rather than a crusader or prophet.

He never enjoyed Congress when he served in it. It was too provincial and gave too little free scope to the individual member who wanted to rise. He was a natural executive. During his administration Congress was largely unfriendly to his New Frontier legislative proposals. Much of this was not his fault. The supporting votes were too often not there. However, many observers have speculated that his heart was not in the leadership of Congress. He was more interested in foreign affairs, an area in which he had more control. He did not find Congressional personalities congenial. He was too much a rationalist to appeal to congressmen in terms of their own perspectives. He had little skill at elaborate legislative strategies. He used the standard techniques but some felt he did so too mechanically and without artistic flair. These hypotheses deserve examination in light of the suggested relationship between the ability to lead Congress and the need for personal power.

His chief strength was administration. His driving energy, rational intelligence, and conception of the Presidency served him well. He cut back the institutionalization of the White House and personally dipped into administration at many levels. He read much and sought information from many sources. Gradually, through trial and error, he developed a system of relying on key subordinates to enhance his power over key decisions. This entire system of control and implementation was shown at its very best in the efficient response of the government to the Cuban missile crisis. Kennedy ran the entire operation himself.

Kennedy as President was intelligent and energetic. His conception of the Presidency and his drive for decisions were great virtues. But perhaps his lack of the needs for attention and power were handicaps to him. This is only a hypothesis to be examined.

Lyndon Johnson seems to have wanted power and influence over others for as long as anyone can remember. He is a thoroughgoing "political man," who has worked throughout his entire career at mastering the skills by which to manipulate others. As a Congressional secretary, a Congressman, a Senator, and finally Senate majority leader, he worked at the mastery of process rather than at substantive issues.

His mind is highly flexible, operational, empirical, and sensitive to the strengths and weaknesses of others and how they can be used for his own purposes.

His values are those of consensus. As a Texan, he was a broker between the South and other regions in Congress. As President he stresses the importance of national consensus over and above American pluralism. This is an attitude that is congenial to his skills as a broker.

As Senate majority leader he dominated that chamber by a combination of hard work, bargaining ability, persuasive power, willingness to use coercive sanctions, and, perhaps most important, the ability to fit the self-interest of many senators into a common pattern on particular pieces of legislation. Of course, this involved considerable watering down of legislation and the charge was made that Johnson, the broker who liked to manipulate, sought agreement at the expense of substance.

This charge is relevant for his Presidency because he has made it clear that he hopes to be a great President, but the skeptical have asked if his methods are not too geared to the production of minimal agreement to permit great creativity or innovations? This question has yet to be answered.

He has taken an active role as leader of public opinion. He does have the ability to dramatize himself and issues, and it seems to be based on a need for attention similar to Theodore Roosevelt's. He has shown an intense hunger for popularity. In the 1964 election campaign he was badly hurt by the reports of newsmen that the crowds did not love him, and his grandstand campaigning seemed designed in part to prove that this was not the case. Often he would taunt newsmen with the facts of his success with huge crowds.

He seems to have the ability to pursue a strategy of leadership on important issues. In March, 1965, Alabama state police committed violence against civil rights demonstrators in Selma, Alabama, and the scene was recorded on television. Johnson seized that opportunity to go before Congress at night, in a televised address, and ask for a voting rights bill. He put the issue in the context of American history and ideals, identified himself with the civil rights movement, and demanded that Congress act in response to outraged public opinion. His position was a strong one because of the nature of the issue and the recent dramatic events, and he took the opportunity to use his strength to the fullest. What was important for our understanding here was his ability to use the maximum leverage on Congress and to arouse public opinion in terms of American principles. He could not have picked a better case by which to advance the cause of civil rights.

Johnson had considerable success in getting his measures through Congress after Kennedy's death, in part because the measures were those of the dead leader. He was equally successful in the 1965 legislative session because of the large increase of Northern Democrats in the 1964 election. However, in both cases, his own skill at legislative manipulation was a factor. He exploited his close and long-standing ties with Congressional leaders, and he used all the standard manipulations and coercions known. But he also gave Congress a sense of participation in the policymaking process. He knows how to flatter Congressional pride and reward Congressional loyalties. And, beyond this, he has a skill at devising compromises that unite diverse men and groups in terms of the self-interest of each. This strategy has brought the same charge that was made against Johnson's Senate majority leadership, that is, he waters down policy to get agreement.

It is too soon to evaluate Johnson as an administrator. A new President requires considerable time to find his way in his own branch. Johnson is a fiercely energetic worker who makes great demands in time, energy, and loyalty upon his staff and associates. He certainly has a sense of personal power in the Presidency. At times it is argued that his egotism is so immense that it stifles the creativity of those beneath him. It will be interesting to see if the supremely legislative man can change over to an effective administrator.

Johnson seems to have the temperament and skills to be one of the great Presidents. He has the drive for personal power that is required. Much more than either Truman or Kennedy he is a craftsman in the art of influencing men. However, this is precisely his public image and he suffers from the fact. Many people deprecate him as a mere "politician" who is lacking in the dignity necessary to a President. This is the paradox we have been discussing all along. His obvious political skill is too obvious. He does not hide it with non-political qualities as the two Roosevelts and Wilson did.

Our models have certainly not explained these three Presidents but they have perhaps provided a framework for comparative study. It is an open question whether enough can ever be known about Presidential candidates to predict their general level of skill as President. It might be interesting to try to do so.

Personality and Situation

There is a pitfall to the kind of analysis of Presidential actions that has been employed in this study. It can easily overemphasize personality as a determinant of Presidential acts and ignore situational considerations, the advice of others to Presidents, and so forth. This is more of a problem when one is trying to give all the causes of specific past actions. That has not been the central purpose of this study. Rather, we have been concerned with the existence or non-existence of skill. Situational factors influence actions but they are executed with varying degrees of skill and over time, by many cases, one can say whether a leader is skillful or not.

However, skill will not guarantee success in terms of winning approval for one's policy. The record would indicate that the great periods of Presidential leadership have been due as much to favorable situational climates as well as to the skill of Presidents. Wilson, F. D. R., and Truman were in office at times of great popular demand for government action. They rode the tide and took the credit. Theodore Roosevelt and John Kennedy came too soon for these groundswells and their successes, despite their skills, were more modest.

It is doubtful if either Taft or Hoover could have salvaged their situations even if they had been extremely skillful. Taft was fighting against the dominant political movement of his day. Hoover was saddled with the first years of a depression at a time when there was very little knowledge about how to respond. Eisenhower was helped by the climate of his times. The public seemed to want stability and consolidation and he gave it to them. A more vigorous kind of leadership might have failed.

Therefore, it is important to remember that leaders must never be given all the credit for their successes or failures. In fact, the same set of skills may be judged more favorably at one time than another in history. One suspects that Eisenhower could have made the decisions that Truman made and thus left office with a stronger professional reputation, had he been President right after the war. However, in general it is hard to imagine the men studied here being basically different kinds of Presidents than they were, regardless of the situation.

The Future

Our chapter themes have been cumulative. Theodore Roosevelt began the creation of the modern Presidency and Wilson and Franklin Roosevelt completed the task. The Presidents of Restraint resisted many of these trends and added little to the institution itself. It has been suggested that Presidents in this tradition, and particularly conservative Presidents, are not at home in the White House because the office has become the agency of popular reform, and the catalyst to government action.

Does this mean that all modern Presidents should be Democrats, that is, Presidents of Action? I would hope not. The Republican Party must develop greater respect for political skill in the Presidency. There is a great need for a definition of skillful Presidential leadership in terms of conservative values. Of course, the Republican Party could make itself over in the liberal image of the Democrats but this seems unlikely. A moderate ideology will have to be developed by leaders who can bring clear skills to the Presidency, not just the anti-skills of the three Presidents of Restraint.

However, for this to happen, the American public will have to be disabused of the notion that a politician in the White House is something of a scandal. We need expert politicians in the Presidency more than ever. It is only through politics that a democratic nation can be governed.